Afghanistan: Narcotics and U.S. Policy

Christopher M. Blanchard
Analyst in Middle Eastern Affairs

August 12, 2009

Congressional Research Service

7-5700
www.crs.gov
RL32686

Summary

Opium poppy cultivation and drug trafficking have eroded Afghanistan's fragile political and economic order over the last 30 years. In spite of ongoing counternarcotics efforts by the Afghan government, the United States, and their partners, Afghanistan remains the source of over 90% of the world's illicit opium. Since 2001, efforts to provide viable economic alternatives to poppy cultivation and to disrupt drug trafficking and related corruption have succeeded in some areas. However, insecurity, particularly in the southern province of Helmand, and widespread corruption fueled a surge in cultivation in 2006 and 2007, pushing opium output to all-time highs. In 2008, poppy cultivation decreased in north-central and eastern Afghanistan, while drug activity became more concentrated in the south and west. National poppy cultivation and opium production totals dropped slightly in 2008, as pressure from provincial officials, higher wheat prices, drought, and lower opium prices altered the cultivation decisions of some Afghan poppy farmers. Some experts have questioned the sustainability of rapid changes in cultivation patterns and recommend reinforcing recent reductions to replace poppy cultivation over time.

Across Afghanistan, insurgents, criminal organizations, and corrupt officials exploit narcotics as a reliable source of revenue and patronage, which has perpetuated the threat these groups pose to the country's fragile internal security and the legitimacy of its democratic government. United Nations officials estimated that the export value of the 2008 opium poppy crop and its derived opiates reached over $3 billion, sustaining fears that Afghanistan's economic recovery continues to be underwritten by drug profits. The trafficking of Afghan drugs also appears to provide financial and logistical support to a range of extremist groups that continue to operate in and around Afghanistan, including resurgent Taliban fighters and some Al Qaeda operatives. Although coalition forces may be less frequently relying on figures involved with narcotics for intelligence and security support, many observers have warned that drug-related corruption among appointed and elected Afghan officials creates political obstacles to progress.

President Obama stated in March 2009 that Afghanistan's "economy is undercut by a booming narcotics trade that encourages criminality and funds the insurgency." Afghan President Hamid Karzai has identified the opium economy as "the single greatest challenge to the long-term security, development, and effective governance of Afghanistan." Congress appropriated approximately $2.9 billion in regular and supplemental counternarcotics foreign assistance and defense funding for Afghanistan programs from FY2001 through FY2009. In March 2009, Obama Administration Special Representative for Afghanistan and Pakistan Ambassador Richard Holbrooke called U.S. counternarcotics efforts in Afghanistan to date "the most wasteful and ineffective program I have seen in 40 years in and out of the government." The Obama Administration and Members of the 111th Congress may consider options for reorganizing counternarcotics efforts as part of new efforts to stabilize Afghanistan.

This report provides current statistical information, profiles the narcotics trade's participants, explores linkages between narcotics, insecurity, and corruption, and reviews U.S. and international policy responses since late 2001. The report also considers ongoing policy debates regarding the counternarcotics role of coalition military forces, poppy eradication, alternative livelihoods, and funding issues for Congress. See also CRS Report RL30588, *Afghanistan: Post-Taliban Governance, Security, and U.S. Policy*, by Kenneth Katzman and CRS Report R40156, *War in Afghanistan: Strategy, Military Operations, and Issues for Congress*, by Catherine Dale.

Contents

Figures

Tables

Contacts

Introduction

In spite of ongoing international efforts to combat Afghanistan's narcotics trade, U.N. officials estimate that Afghanistan supplies over 90% of the world's illicit opium.[1] Afghan, U.S., and international officials have stated that opium poppy cultivation and drug trafficking constitute serious strategic threats to the security and stability of Afghanistan and jeopardize the success of post-9/11 counterterrorism and reconstruction efforts. Since 2001, counternarcotics policy has emerged as a focal point in broader, recurring debates in the executive branch and in Congress about the United States' strategic objectives and policies in Afghanistan.

Relevant concerns include the role of U.S. military personnel and strategies for continuing the simultaneous pursuit of counterterrorism and counternarcotics goals, which may be complicated by practical necessities and political realities. Coalition forces pursuing regional security and counterterrorism objectives may rely on the cooperation of security commanders, tribal leaders, and local officials who may be involved in the narcotics trade. Similarly, U.S. officials and many observers believe that the introduction of a democratic system of government to Afghanistan has been accompanied by the election and appointment of narcotics-associated individuals to positions of public office.

Efforts to combat the opium trade in Afghanistan face the challenge of ending a highly-profitable enterprise fueled by international demand that has become deeply interwoven with the economic, political, and social fabric of a war-torn country. Afghan, U.S., and international authorities are engaged in a campaign to reverse the unprecedented upsurge of opium poppy cultivation and heroin production that occurred following the fall of the Taliban. U.S. officials continue to implement a multifaceted counternarcotics initiative that includes public awareness campaigns, judicial reform measures, economic and agricultural development assistance, drug interdiction operations, and more robust poppy eradication. The Obama Administration and the 111th Congress may consider options for modifying U.S. counternarcotics efforts in Afghanistan in order to meet the challenges posed by the Afghan opium economy to the security of Afghanistan and the international community. Questions regarding the likely effectiveness, resource requirements, and implications of new counternarcotics strategies in Afghanistan may arise during the first session of the 111th Congress as such options are debated.

Afghanistan's Opium Economy

Opium production has become an entrenched negative element of Afghanistan's fragile political and economic order over the last 30 years in spite of ongoing local, regional, and international efforts to reverse its growth. At the time of Afghanistan's pro-Communist coup in 1978, narcotics experts estimated that Afghan farmers produced 300 metric tons (MT) of opium annually, enough to satisfy most local and regional demand and to supply a handful of heroin production facilities whose products were bound for Western Europe.[2] Since the 1980s, a trend of increasing opium

---

[1] United Nations Office on Drugs and Crime (UNODC)/Government of Afghanistan Ministry of Counternarcotics (MCN), *Afghan Opium Survey 2008*, November 2008.

[2] See Jonathan C. Randal, "Afghanistan's Promised War on Opium," *Washington Post*, November 2, 1978, and Stuart Auerbach, "New Heroin Connection: Afghanistan and Pakistan Supply West With Opium," *Washington Post*, October 11, 1979.

---

poppy cultivation and opium production has unfolded during successive periods of insurgency, civil war, fundamentalist government, and recently, international engagement (**Figures 1** and **2**). During the 2006-2007 poppy growing season, Afghanistan produced a world record opium poppy crop that yielded 8,200 MT of illicit opium—an estimated 93% of the world's supply. A slight reduction in national poppy cultivation and opium output was recorded in 2007-2008, and many international officials attributed the changes to more effective counternarcotics approaches, including governor-enforced poppy cultivation bans and eradication.

While annual, nationwide statistics often dominate media coverage and policy debates, some experts argue that policy makers and legislators seeking to create durable and sustainable reductions in poppy cultivation and drug trafficking should observe regional and local changes over time. For example, experienced Afghanistan field researchers David Mansfield and Adam Pain argue in a December 2008 report that policy makers should examine the economic, political, and social factors that change cultivation patterns at sub national levels in order to tailor policy responses in a way that builds on incremental local successes and development.[3] Observers who have expressed similar views have argued for more targeted and integrated use of the development assistance, eradication, interdiction, and public outreach approaches currently in use rather than calling for the employment of entirely new methods or strategies.

Overall, practitioners and observers remained focused on Afghan government, United Nations, and other field reporting that shows reductions in poppy cultivation in some northern, central, and eastern provinces, while large-scale cultivation continues in conflict-ridden southern provinces and remote areas of the east and west. By nearly all accounts, opiate trafficking and related corruption remain nationwide problems. With regard to so-called "poppy free" provinces, experts and practitioners continue to debate the causes and durability of recent reductions in poppy cultivation, with some analysts calling for more targeted development assistance to capitalize on and consolidate what they argue are still-reversible reductions. Parallel debates focus on the advisability and targeting of interdiction and eradication and the relative importance of and appropriate methods for sustainably replacing poppy as an income source for Afghan households.

In the most volatile areas of the country, insecurity and corruption create a climate in which poppy cultivators and drug trafficking groups remain largely free to operate. Violence and criminality stifle licit economic activity and prevent effective eradication, interdiction, outside investment, or the provision of development assistance. Reports suggest that the drug trade provides financial support to corrupt officials, criminal groups, and insurgents who in turn protect traffickers and perpetuate the chaotic environments that allow illicit trade to thrive. In light of these challenges, current policy efforts seek to understand, consolidate, and sustain reductions in cultivation where they have occurred and to break self-reinforcing cycles of insecurity, crime, and violence through direct action against traffickers, insurgents, and corrupt officials.

---

[3] Mansfield and Pain argue that "...one year's measure of opium area cannot assess trends of long term change nor does it reveal how any change occurred or, therefore, the likely sustainability of that change. ... Measures of positive changes in security, economic growth and governance — together with declines in hectarage — better reflect a more sustainable shift out of opium poppy cultivation and progress towards the achievement of counter-narcotics outcomes. More appropriate measures for judging progress in the short and medium term might be improvements in rural livelihood security associated with basic security; social protection, including the achievement of food security; and economic growth." David Mansfield and Adam Pain, "Counter-Narcotics in Afghanistan: The Failure of Success?" *Afghanistan Research and Evaluation Unit* (Kabul), Briefing Paper Series, December 2008. Available at: http://www.areu.org.af/index.php?option=com_docman&Itemid=26&task=doc_download&gid=617.

Current Production Statistics

According to the 2008 Afghanistan Opium Survey conducted by the UNODC and the Afghan Ministry of Counternarcotics (MCN):

- Opium poppy cultivation took place in 16 of 34 Afghan provinces in 2007-2008 (see **Figure 3**). The land area under poppy cultivation fell by 19% to 157,000 hectares (equal to 2.1% of Afghanistan's arable land). Cultivation has become overwhelmingly concentrated in conflict-ridden Helmand province, where farmers cultivated over 103,000 hectares of poppy—66% of the national total and an area greater than any nationwide cultivation total prior to 2004. The U.S. Central Intelligence Agency Crime and Narcotics Center estimated that 116,365 hectares were cultivated in 2008, down from 140,600 hectares in 2007.[4]

- The 2007-2008 opium poppy crop produced 7,700 MT of illicit opium, a 6% decline from the prior season. However, crop yields improved 15% due to better weather conditions in some areas. A range of accepted opium to heroin conversion rates indicate that this year's estimated opium yield of 7,700 MT could produce 770 to 1160 MT of refined heroin.[5]

- Approximately 366,500 Afghan families cultivated opium poppy in 2007-2008, a 28% decrease from 2006 and equal to roughly 2.4 million people or 10% of the Afghan population. In 2005, 2 million people or 8.7% of the population were estimated to have cultivated poppy. Thousands of laborers and an unknown number of traffickers, warlords, and officials continue to participate.

- The estimated $700 million farmgate value (equal to volume multiplied by the price of non-dried opium paid to farmers) of the 2007-2008 opium harvest is equivalent in value to approximately 7% of the country's licit GDP. The export value may exceed $3.4 billion, equivalent to approximately 33% of the country's licit GDP. Many licit and emerging industries have been financed or supported by profits from narcotics trafficking.[6]

As noted above, some experts and practitioners consider provincial and district level data to be a more accurate reflection of counternarcotics challenges and successes. Recent UNODC/MCN reports attribute sustainable declines in poppy cultivation to political stability, economic integration, alternative livelihood assistance, and effective forced eradication. Other variables such as weather, raw opium prices (see **Table 1**), and the prices of licit crops have significant and difficult to quantify effects on farmers' decisions to cultivate poppy over time.

---

[4] Questions for the Record, Senator John Kerry, Nomination of Hillary Rodham Clinton, Department of State, Secretary of State, released January 13, 2009. U.S. government agencies use different methodologies and technologies to derive cultivation and production estimates; U.S. estimates are generally lower than Afghan government and UNODC estimates.

[5] Methodology described in UNODC/Afghan Gov., Afghanistan Opium Survey 2004, November 2004, pp. 105-7.

[6] Edouard Martin and Steven Symansky, "Macroeconomic Impact of the Drug Economy and Counter-Narcotics Efforts," in Doris Buddenberg and William A. Byrd (eds.), *Afghanistan's Drug Industry: Structure, Functioning, Dynamics, and Implications for Counter-Narcotics Policy*, World Bank/UNODC, November 2006.

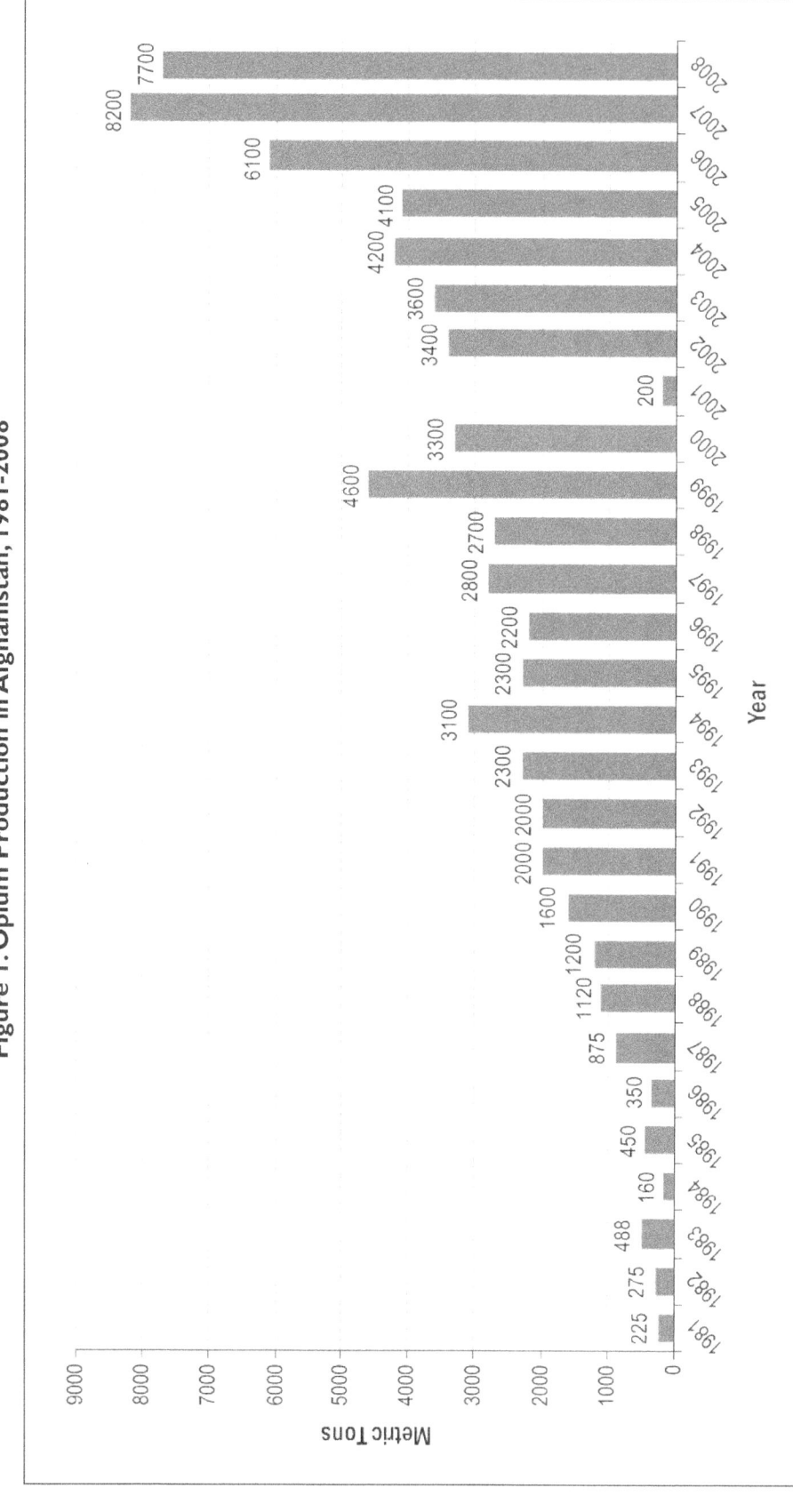

Figure 1. Opium Production in Afghanistan, 1981-2008

Source: Graphic developed by CRS using UNODC/MCN data. One metric ton is equal to 2,200 pounds. The Taliban banned opium poppy cultivation in areas under their control in 2001 but allowed opium trafficking to continue. Limited poppy cultivation continued in areas under Northern Alliance control.

Figure 2. Opium Poppy Cultivation in Afghanistan, 1986-2008

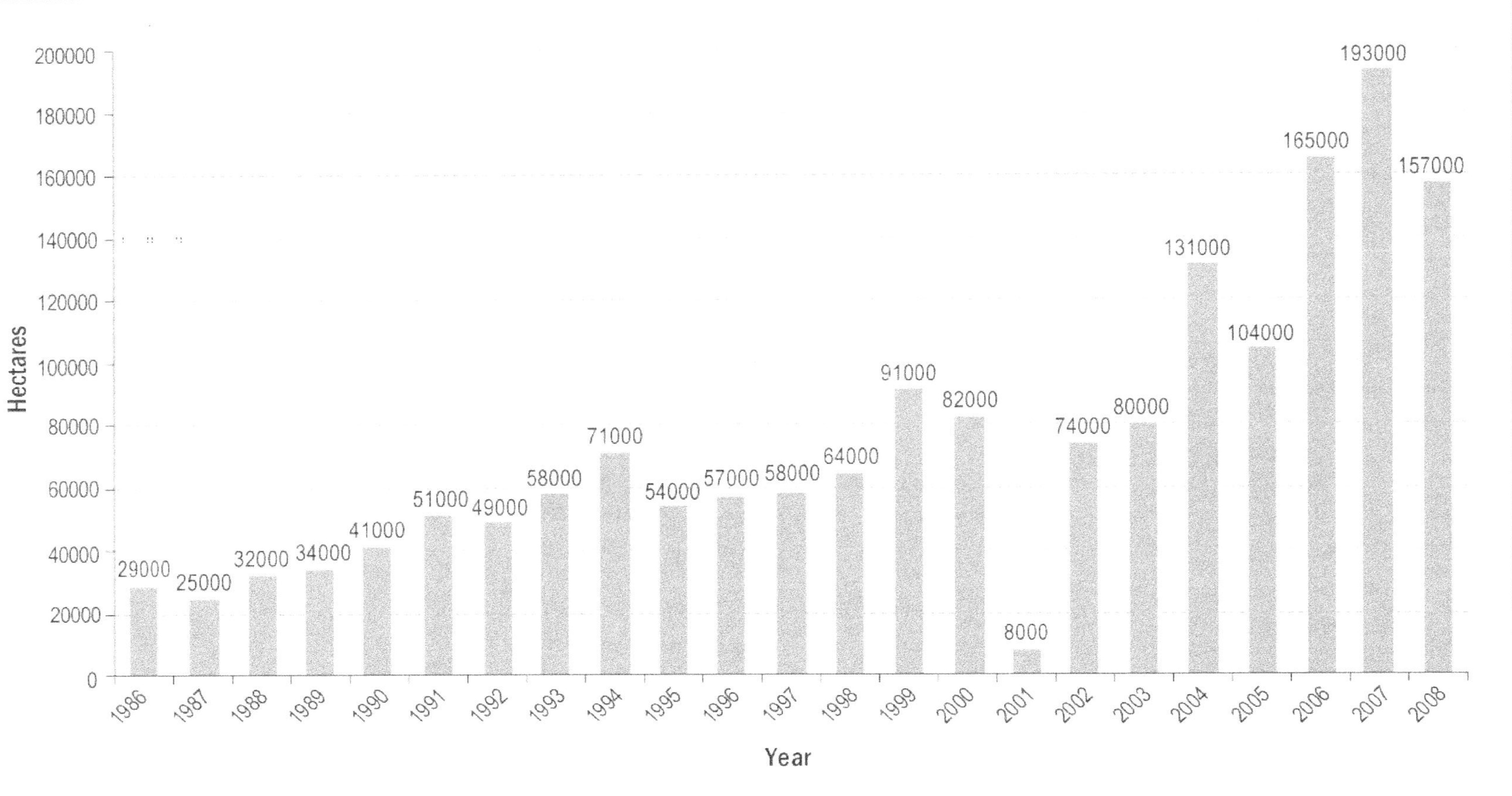

Year	Hectares
1986	29000
1987	25000
1988	32000
1989	34000
1990	41000
1991	51000
1992	49000
1993	58000
1994	71000
1995	54000
1996	57000
1997	58000
1998	64000
1999	91000
2000	82000
2001	8000
2002	74000
2003	80000
2004	131000
2005	104000
2006	165000
2007	193000
2008	157000

Source: Graphic developed by CRS using UNODC/MCN data. One hectare is equal to 10,000 square meters. The Taliban banned opium poppy cultivation in areas under their control in 2001 but allowed opium trafficking to continue. Limited poppy cultivation continued in areas under Northern Alliance control.

Figure 3. Estimated Opium Poppy Cultivation by District, 2008

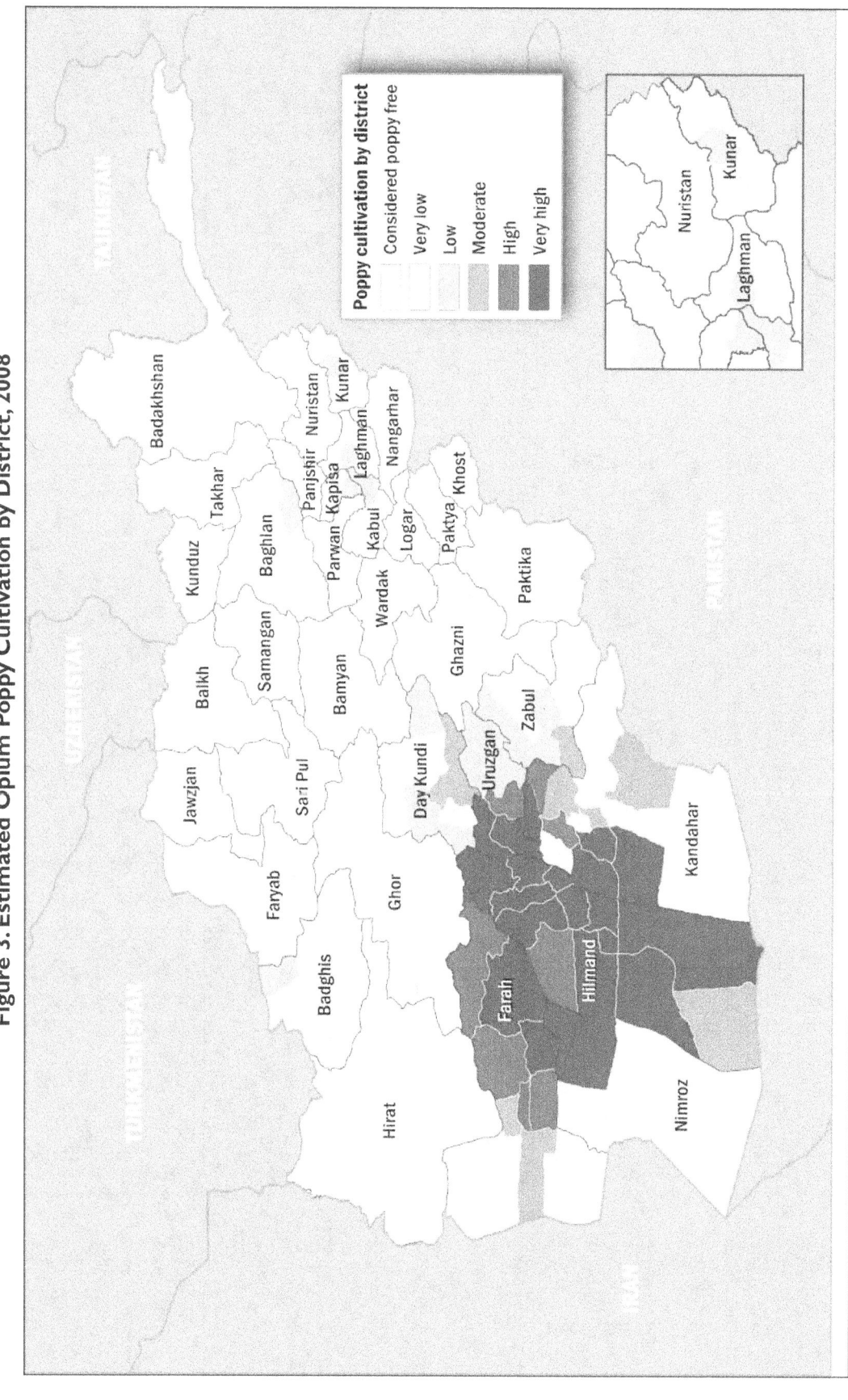

Source: Adapted by CRS from UNODC/MCN Afghanistan Opium Survey 2008, p. 36.

Notes: District boundaries approximate.

Table 1. Opium Prices in Afghanistan

(regionally weighted fresh opium farmgate[a] price, current US$/kilogram)

	2000	2001[b]	2002	2003	2004	2005	2006	2007	2008	2009[c]
Opium Price	$28	$301	$350	$283	$92	$102	$94	$86	$70	$55

Source: United Nations Office on Drugs and Crime, Afghanistan Opium Surveys 2004-2008; and, Winter Rapid Assessment, January 2009

a. Farmgate price for fresh opium is the price paid to farmers for non-dried opium.

b. Dry opium prices increase following the Taliban ban on poppy cultivation and skyrocketed to nearly $700/kg immediately following the September 11, 2001 terrorist attacks. According to UNODC, prices temporarily fell to $93/kg after U.S. airstrikes began.

c. UNODC reported price as of November 2008.

UNODC Projections and U.S. Assessments, 2009[7]

The January 2009 UNODC winter opium assessment predicts further consolidation of poppy cultivation in the southern and western provinces of Helmand, Kandahar, Nimroz, Farah, Dai Kundi, Uruzgan, and Zabol. Over 90% of Afghanistan's opium will likely be produced in these seven provinces, according to UNODC. Nevertheless, UNODC expects "some decrease" in overall cultivation and suggests that four provinces, Herat, Baghlan, Faryab, and Badakhshan, could become "poppy-free" in 2009. Higher prices for crops such as wheat, lower opium prices, pressure from government officials, and the persistence of drought are credited as encouraging farmers to concentrate limited resources into the cultivation of non-poppy crops. Survey data suggests that government intervention remains less influential in southern and western provinces, although Afghan media reports suggest that eradication and interdiction operations were taking place across southern Afghanistan in early 2009. Farmers surveyed also suggested that the effectiveness of alternative development programs varies across the country, and many reportedly emphasized the need for programs to extend beyond district centers to more remote or "grass roots" areas.

The 2009 State Department International Narcotics Control Strategy Report for Afghanistan states that:

> "the Government of the Islamic Republic of Afghanistan (GIRoA) generally cooperates with the international community in implementing its national counternarcotics strategy. However, more political will and effort, at the central and provincial levels, is required to decrease cultivation in the south, maintain cultivation reductions in the rest of the country, and combat trafficking in coming years."

The report also concludes that "the Afghan government has been unwilling or unable to fully implement [its National Drug Control Strategy] and has, in some cases, failed to provide adequate support to provincial leaders who have shown greater willingness to take serious steps to combat narcotics cultivation, production, and trafficking in their provinces." In April 2009, Secretary of State Hillary Clinton called corruption in Afghanistan "a cancer" that "eats away at the

---

[7] Based on UNODC/MCN, Afghanistan Opium Winter Rapid Assessment, January 2009.

confidence and the trust of the people in their government."[8] The 2009 INCSR report concludes that "many Afghan government officials are believed to profit from the drug trade," and "narcotics-related corruption is particularly pervasive at the provincial and district levels of government."[9]

Obama Administration Strategic Review and Funding Requests

According to U.S. officials, strategic guidance outlined in 2007 (see "U.S. Policy Initiatives: Transition from the "Five-Pillar" Plan" below) will continue to shape ongoing programs until the Obama Administration begins implementing new policies in conjunction with its strategic reviews of U.S. policy in Afghanistan and Pakistan. The Administration's strategic review white paper, released March 27, 2009, calls for "a complete overhaul of our civilian assistance strategy" and identifies "agricultural sector job creation" as "an essential first step to undercutting the appeal of al Qaeda and its allies." The review document states that the Obama Administration believes crop substitution and alternative livelihood programs in Afghanistan "have been disastrously underdeveloped and under-resourced." It further indicates that interdiction and eradication operations will continue, but targeting will shift toward "higher level drug lords."

In support of these objectives, the Administration is requesting civilian staff funding, development assistance, and enforcement funding in the FY2009 supplemental and its FY2010 budget proposal. The FY2009 supplemental request includes Diplomatic and Consular Program funding requests for $84.8 million to support new U.S. Embassy and provincial reconstruction team (PRT) personnel from the State Department, USAID, and the U.S. Department of Agriculture (USDA). In addition, the D&CP account request includes $137.6 million to support expanded interagency staffing in the areas of agriculture, justice, customs and border management, health, finance, and aviation. Some of the staffing funding requests will directly increase the number of U.S. personnel devoted to counternarcotics programs in Afghanistan. The Administration also is requesting $129 million in International Narcotics Control and Law Enforcement (INCLE) account funding to "support counternarcotics and law enforcement efforts primarily in the south and east of Afghanistan" and $214 million in Economic Support Fund (ESF) account funding to support "counternarcotics and stabilization programs, especially in the south and east." The Administration's FY2010 request does not dramatically expand economic assistance specifically earmarked for counternarcotics purposes, in spite of official statements about those programs having been "under-resourced" in the past. However, ESF assistance requests for agricultural programs are significantly larger for FY2010.

Table 2 details appropriations and requests for the main funding accounts supporting U.S. counternarcotics programming in Afghanistan for FY2007 through FY2010. Drug Enforcement Administration (DEA) funds are not included. The Special Inspector General for Afghanistan Reconstruction (SIGAR) estimates that Congress appropriated approximately $3 billion for counternarcotics programs in Afghanistan from 2001 through 2008. Since 2006, Congress has placed conditions on some amounts of U.S. economic assistance to Afghanistan by requiring the President to certify that the Afghan government is cooperating fully with counternarcotics efforts prior to the obligation of funds or to issue a national security waiver (see "Certification Requirements" below).

---

[8] Radio Free Europe/Radio Liberty, Full Transcript Of Interview With Hillary Clinton, April 6, 2009.

[9] Available at: http://www.state.gov/p/inl/rls/nrcrpt/2009/vol1/116520.htm.

Table 2. U.S. Counternarcotics Appropriations and Requests, Afghanistan FY2007-FY2010

(Current $, millions)

Account[a]	FY2007		FY2008			FY2009 Estimate			FY2010 Request
	Base	Supplemental	Base	Bridge	Supplemental	Base	Bridge	Supplemental Request	Base Request
International Narcotics Control and Law Enforcement (INCLE)	169.74	27.00	204.13	-	8.00	216.00	46.00	49.00	288.23
Economic Support Funds (ESF)	64.95	155.00	81.66	-	65.00	61.60	38.00	214.00[b]	185.00
Development Assistance (DA)	9.00	-	30.39	-	-	-	-	-	-
Department of Defense Counterdrug Activities[c]	112.90[d]	178.00	20.65	105.57	63.40	21.40	150.30	141.20[b]	324.60[e]
Total	**$716.59**		**$578.80**			**$937.50**			**$797.83**

Source: U.S. Department of State, Congressional Budget Justifications for Foreign Operations Requests; U.S. Department of Defense - Office of the Undersecretary of Defense (Comptroller), Justification Materials; and, CRS communications with Office of the Secretary of Defense and Department of State Bureau of Legislative Affairs, 2007 through June 2009. FY2009 totals are estimates pending the completion of consultations between congressional appropriations committees and the executive branch.

Notes:

a. Figures for State Department administered accounts (INCLE, ESF, DA) for FY2006 to FY2010 (including base request and bridge appropriation) reflect amounts designated for the 'Counternarcotics' program area, under the 'Peace and Security' objective in the State Department's foreign assistance framework. Other funds appropriated in those and other accounts also may contribute to the achievement of U.S. counternarcotics objectives. For more information on the State Department foreign assistance framework, see CRS Report R40213, *Foreign Aid: An Introduction to U.S. Programs and Policy*, by Curt Tarnoff and Marian Leonardo Lawson.

b. The FY 2009 ESF account Supplemental Request figure reflects the full amount designated for the 'Peace and Security' objective under the State Department's foreign assistance framework. Justification material suggests that some of this requested total will support the "Counternarcotics" program area, but other funds will support stability operations that may contribute to counternarcotics objectives. Final ESF account totals will be determined by congressional appropriations committees and the executive branch. The Department of Defense FY2009 supplemental request figure funds activities "related to Afghanistan, Central Asia, and the Horn of Africa."

c. Figures for Department of Defense Counterdrug Activities denote total funds used for programs in Afghanistan only, unless otherwise noted.

d. Included $100 million in Title IX funds provided by the conference report on H.R. 5631 (H.Rept. 109-676).

e. Reflects worldwide total designated for FY2010 Overseas Contingency Operations - Counterdrug Activities. Country breakdown not available as of August 12, 2009.

Table 3. Defense Department Use of FY2008 Regular, Bridge, and Supplemental Drug Interdiction and Counterdrug Funds

(Current $, million)

Proposed Purpose	FY2008 Defense Appropriation P.L. 110-116	FY2008 Bridge Fund P.L. 110-161 (Division L)	FY2008 Supplemental P.L. 110-252 (Title IX, Chapter 1)	Total
National Interdiction Unit (NIU), Counternarcotics Police of Afghanistan (CNPA) Support	12.696	69.319	8.454	**$90.469**
Counternarcotics Border Police Support	-	15.692	16.246	**$31.938**
Intelligence and Technology Efforts	3.950	17.675	35.700	**$57.325**
Other Program Support	4.000	2.887	3.000	**$9.887**
Pakistan Special Services Group, and Frontier Corps Support	-	54.675	-	**$54.675**
Other Nation Support [CENTCOM AOR]	4.322[a]	32.353	1.600	**$33.953**
Total	**$24.968**	**$192.601**	**$65.000**	**$282.569**

Source: Office of the Secretary of Defense communication to CRS, December 30, 2008.

a. Includes appropriated funds planned for use in Turkmenistan, Krygyzstan, Tajikistan, Kazakhstan, and "other regional support" in the CENTCOM area of responsibility.

Table 4. Defense Department Planned Use of FY2009 Base Appropriation and Bridge Drug Interdiction and Counterdrug Funds

(Current $, million)

Proposed Purpose	FY2009 Defense Appropriation P.L. 110-329 (Division C)	FY2009 Bridge Fund P.L. 110-252 (Title IX, Ch. 2)	Total
National Interdiction Unit (NIU), Counternarcotics Police of Afghanistan (CNPA) Support	13.622	66.171	**$79.793**
Counternarcotics Border Police Support	3.812	27.309	**$31.121**
Intelligence and Technology Efforts	4.000	41.750	**$45.750**
Other Program Support	-	15.070	**$15.070**
Pakistan Coast Guard, Special Services Group, and Frontier Corps Support	-	37.450	**$37.450**
Other CENTCOM AOR Support	6.240[a]	0.250	**$0.259**
Total	**$27.674**	**$188.000**	**$215.674**

Source: Office of the Secretary of Defense communication to CRS, June 18, 2009.

a. Includes appropriated funds planned for use in Turkmenistan, Krygyzstan, Tajikistan, and "other regional support" in the CENTCOM area of responsibility.

Issues for Congress

Experts and government officials have warned that narcotics trafficking jeopardizes international efforts to secure and stabilize Afghanistan. U.S. officials believe that efforts to reverse the related trends of opium cultivation, drug trafficking, corruption, and insecurity must expand if broader strategic objectives are to be achieved. A broad U.S. interagency initiative to assist Afghan authorities in combating the narcotics trade has been developed, and some officials argue that the U.S. efforts have been effective in areas where all elements of the strategy have been advanced simultaneously. However, in many areas, regional insecurity and corruption continue to prevent or complicate counternarcotics initiatives and thus present formidable challenges.

Primary issues of interest to the Congress include program funding, the role of the U.S. military, and the scope and nature of eradication and development assistance initiatives. During the term of the 110th Congress, the Bush Administration argued that insecurity in key opium poppy producing areas, delays in building and reforming Afghan institutions, and widespread Afghan corruption continued to prevent full implementation of U.S. and Afghan counternarcotics strategies. The Obama Administration and the 111th Congress may seek to further amend existing strategies and programs in line with the recommendations of recently completed policy reviews.

Breaking the Narcotics-Insecurity Cycle

Narcotics trafficking and political instability remain intimately linked in Afghanistan. U.S. officials have identified narcotics trafficking as a primary barrier to the establishment of security and consider insecurity to be a primary barrier to successful counternarcotics operations. The narcotics-trade fuels three corrosive trends that have undermined the stability of Afghan society and limited progress toward reconstruction since 2001. First, narcotics proceeds can corrupt police, judges, and government officials and prevent the establishment of basic rule of law in many areas. Second, the narcotics trade can provide the Taliban and other insurgents with funding and arms that support their violent activities. Third, corruption and violence can prevent reform and development necessary for the renewal of legitimate economic activity. In the most conflict-prone areas, symbiotic relationships between narcotics producers, traffickers, insurgents, and corrupt officials can create self-reinforcing cycles of violence and criminality (see **Figure 4**) Across Afghanistan, the persistence of these trends undermines Afghan civilians' confidence in their local, provincial, and national government institutions.

Critics of existing counternarcotics efforts have argued that Afghan authorities and their international partners remain reluctant to directly confront prominent individuals and groups involved in the opium trade because of their fear that confrontation will lead to internal security disruptions or expand armed conflict to include drug-related groups. In the past, Afghan authorities have expressed their belief that "the beneficiaries of the drugs trade will resist attempts to destroy it," and have argued that "the political risk of internal instability caused by counternarcotics measures" must be balanced "with the requirement to project central authority nationally" for counternarcotics purposes.[10] To date, conflict and regional security disruptions have accompanied efforts to expand crop eradication programs and previous efforts to implement central government counternarcotics policies.

---

[10] National Drug Control Strategy, Transitional Islamic State of Afghanistan, May 18, 2003.

Figure 4. Narcotics, Corruption, and Security in Afghanistan

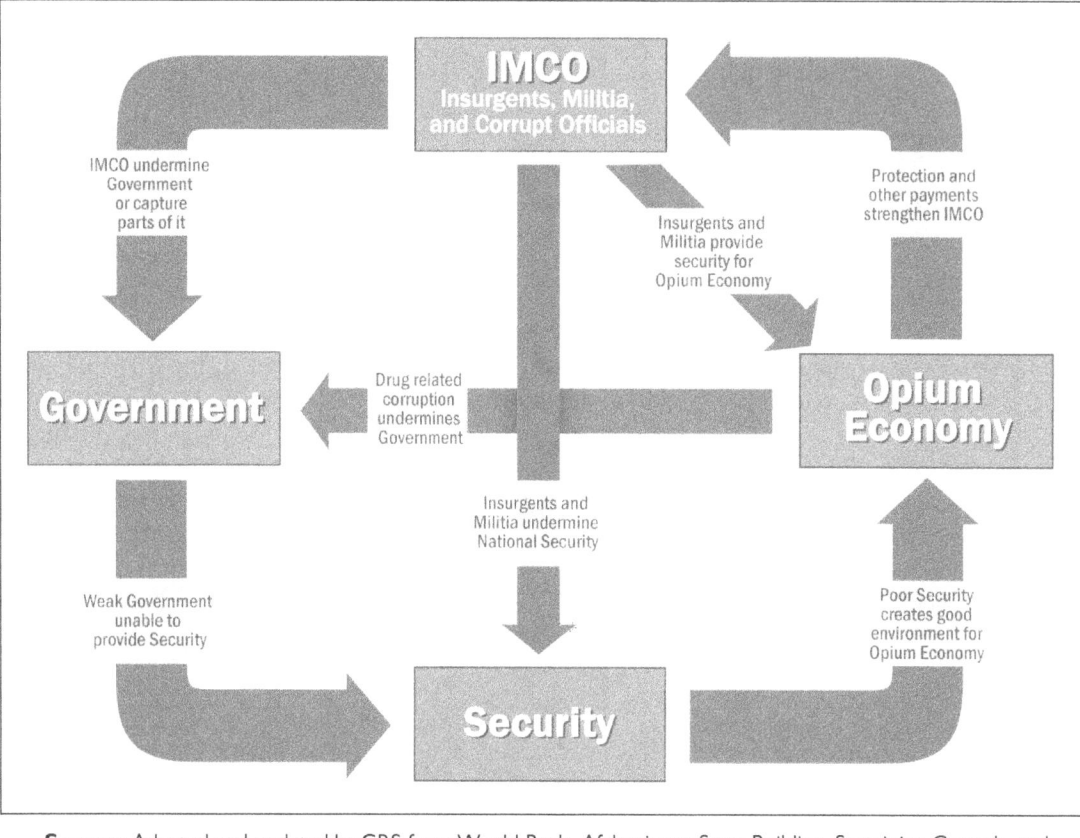

Source: Adapted and updated by CRS from World Bank, Afghanistan: State Building, Sustaining Growth, and Reducing Poverty, Country Economic Report No. 29551-AF September 9, 2004, p. 87.

For years, U.S. officials have identified rural security and national rule of law as prerequisites for effective counternarcotics policy implementation, while simultaneously identifying narcotics as a primary threat to security and stability. As early as 2005, the State Department was arguing that:

> "Poppy cultivation is likely to continue until responsible governmental authority is established throughout the country and until rural poverty levels can be reduced via provision of alternative livelihoods and increased rural incomes.... Drug processing and trafficking can be expected to continue until security is established and drug law enforcement capabilities can be increased."[11]

Although an increasing number of Afghan police, security forces, and counternarcotics authorities are being trained by U.S. and coalition officials, the size and capability of Afghan forces may limit their power to effectively challenge entrenched drug trafficking groups and regional militia in the short term. Specifically, questions remain as to whether Afghan security and counternarcotics forces alone will be able to establish the security conditions necessary for the more robust interdiction and alternative livelihood programs planned by U.S. and Afghan officials. The establishment of the Afghan National Army's Counternarcotics Infantry Kandak in 2008 and the deployment of eradication teams to Helmand, Kandahar, and Uruzgan province in early 2009 indicate that some steps have been taken to address these challenges, although the

---

[11] Department of State, INCSR, March 2005.

future of U.S. assistance to Afghan eradication activities appears limited based on statements from Obama Administration officials.

From a political perspective, U.S. officials maintain that parliamentary and provincial elections have contributed to the political legitimacy of the central government and, by extension, its counternarcotics initiatives. However, the creation of sufficient political and military stability for effective counternarcotics operations is likely to remain a significant challenge. Local police, local officials, and border police are considered to be the best positioned to create conditions of security necessary for "full spectrum" counternarcotics activity. They also are considered to be the most susceptible to and compromised by narcotics-related corruption. The death of several local contractor employees working on USAID alternative livelihood projects in May 2005 brought renewed urgency to concerns about the provision of security as a prerequisite for non-enforcement related counternarcotics programs. These concerns may return to the forefront of congressional debate as U.S. counterinsurgency efforts target remaining areas of widespread poppy cultivation in the most insecure areas of the country and seek to expand development assistance programs.

Balancing Counterterrorism, Counterinsurgency, and Counternarcotics

In pursuing counterterrorism and counterinsurgency objectives, Afghan and coalition authorities consider difficult political choices when confronting corrupt officials, militia leaders, and narcotics traffickers. Regional and local militia commanders with alleged links to the opium trade played significant roles in coalition efforts to undermine the Taliban regime and capture Al Qaeda operatives, particularly in southern and southeastern Afghanistan.[12] Some of these figures and their political allies have been incorporated into government and security structures, including positions of responsibility for enforcing counternarcotics policies.[13] For example, the current governor of Nangarhar province, Gul Agha Sherzai, is now credited with effectively enforcing bans on poppy cultivation and supporting anti-drug trafficking efforts. However, in 2001 and 2002, as governor of his native Kandahar province, he was alleged to have maintained a close relationship with an alleged Taliban-associated narcotics kingpin that has been indicted on drug trafficking charges in the United States (see "Taliban and Insurgent Groups" below).[14]

Pragmatic decisions taken since 2001 to prioritize counterterrorism operations and current plans to employ counterinsurgency tactics against the Taliban and enforce counternarcotics policies

---

[12] According to Afghanistan scholar Barnett Rubin, "the empowerment and enrichment of the warlords who allied with the United States in the anti-Taliban efforts, and whose weapons and authority now enabled them to tax and protect opium traffickers," have provided the opium trade "with powerful new protectors." Rubin, "Road to Ruin: Afghanistan's Booming Opium Industry," October 7, 2004.

[13] See Syed Saleem Shahzad, "U.S. Turns to Drug Baron to Rally Support," *Asia Times*, December 4, 2001; Charles Clover and Peronet Despeignes, "Murder Undermines Karzai Government," *Financial Times*, July 8, 2002; Susan B. Glasser, "U.S. Backing Helps Warlord Solidify Power," *Washington Post*, February 18, 2002; Ron Moreau and Sami Yousafzai, with Donatella Lorch, "Flowers of Destruction," *Newsweek*, July 14, 2003; Andrew North, "Warlord Tells Police Chief to Go," *BBC News*, July 12, 2004; Steven Graham, "Group: Warlords to Hinder Afghan Election," *Associated Press*, September 28, 2004; and Anne Barnard and Farah Stockman, "U.S. Weighs Role in Heroin War in Afghanistan," *Boston Globe*, October 20, 2004.

[14] *CBS Evening News*, "Newly Arrived US Army Soldiers Find it Difficult to Adjust...." February 7, 2002; Mark Corcoran, "America's Blind Eye," Australian Broadcasting Corporation, *Foreign Correspondent*, April 10, 2002; and, Steve Inskeep, "Afghanistan's Opium Trade," National Public Radio, April 26, 2002.

---

more strictly may conflict with each other, forcing Afghan and coalition authorities to address seemingly difficult contradictions. "Tactical" coalition allies in militia and other irregular forces with ties to the drug trade may inhibit the ability of the central government to extend its authority and enforce its counternarcotics policies.[15] At the same time, U.S. and Afghan officials have been increasingly adamant in stating that the Taliban resurgence that has unfolded since early 2006 has been supported in part by narcotics proceeds and that narcotics related corruption undermines the effectiveness of Afghan security forces.

These issues may weigh strongly in decision concerning the feasibility and prospects for success of continuing U.S. counterterrorism, counterinsurgency, and counternarcotics operations. One senior Defense Department official has argued that U.S. counternarcotics strategy in Afghanistan must recognize "the impact the drug trade has on our other policy objectives, while complementing (and not competing with) our other efforts in furtherance of those objectives."[16] Striking such a balance may continue to create challenges for the United States and its allies.

Defining the Role of the U.S. Military and ISAF

Targeting and Enforcement

For years, some observers have argued that U.S., coalition, and NATO military forces should play an active, direct role in targeting the leaders and infrastructure of the opiate trade. For example, following the announcement of record poppy cultivation and opium production in 2005-2006, UNODC Director Antonio Maria Costa called for direct NATO military involvement in counternarcotics enforcement operations in Afghanistan. Arguments in favor of coalition involvement in counternarcotics enforcement activities often cited the limited capabilities of Afghan security forces and held that coalition forces able take action against narcotics traffickers should do so in the interest of Afghanistan's national security and coalition goals.

In general, opponents of a direct enforcement role for U.S., coalition, or NATO forces have claimed that such a role would alienate forces from the Afghan population, jeopardize ongoing counterterrorism missions that require local Afghan intelligence support, and divert limited coalition military resources from direct counter-insurgent and counterterrorism operations. Others in the U.S. government and in Congress have opposed direct military involvement in counternarcotics enforcement activities based on concerns about maintaining distinct authorities and capabilities among agencies. For example, the House report on the FY2007 Defense authorization bill argued that the Defense Department "must not take on roles in which other countries or other agencies of the U.S. Government have core capabilities" with regard to counternarcotics in Afghanistan.

During the Bush Administration, U.S. Central Command (CENTCOM) officials indicated that Defense Department counternarcotics programs in Afghanistan were "a key element of our campaign against terrorism."[17] However, U.S. military officials largely resisted the establishment

---

[15] The 2007 UNODC Afghanistan Opium Survey argued that "in the provinces bordering with Pakistan, tacit acceptance of opium trafficking by foreign military forces as a way to extract intelligence information and occasional military support in operations against the Taliban and Al-Qaida undermines stabilization efforts."

[16] Testimony of Mary-Beth Long, then-Deputy Assistant Secretary of Defense for Counternarcotics before the House Committee on International Relations, March 17, 2005.

[17] "U.S. CENTCOM views narcotrafficking as a significant obstacle to the political and economic reconstruction of (continued...)

of a direct counternarcotics enforcement role for U.S. forces owing to limited resources and concerns about exacerbating security threats. As late as 2006, former NATO Commander and current National Security Adviser General James Jones advanced the idea that counternarcotics enforcement was "not a military mission," and stated that "having NATO troops out there burning crops" was "not going to significantly contribute to the war on drugs."[18]

Until October 2008, NATO International Security Assistance Force (ISAF) directives precluded direct military action against narcotics targets such as traffickers and laboratories.[19] Changes in authorization agreed to in Budapest during an October 2008 meeting and subsequent consultations now allow ISAF forces to take action against insurgency-linked narcotics targets if they so choose and if authorized under their own domestic laws.[20]

According to the Department of Defense, U.S. military forces have long been authorized to seize narcotics and related supplies encountered during the course of normal stability and counterterrorism operations. Those basic rules of engagement reportedly have been changed, but the Defense Department is not making public any details on the content of reported changes.[21] Defense Department policy guidance issued in December 2008 states that Department personnel "will not directly participate in searches, seizures, arrests, or similar activity unless such personnel are otherwise authorized by law" with the exception of the provision of force protection "up to and including on the objective."[22] According to the guidance, Department personnel may accompany U.S. or host nation law enforcement and security forces on counternarcotics field operations within presidentially declared combat zones. Executive Order 13239 (issued December 12, 2001, effective as of September 19, 2001) designated Afghanistan and the airspace above it as combat zones.[23]

In August 2009, the Senate Foreign Relations Committee released a report containing statements from unnamed U.S. military officers and officials that provides an unconfirmed account of how

---

(...continued)

Afghanistan... Local terrorist and criminal leaders have a vested interest in using the profits from narcotics to oppose the central government and undermine the security and stability of Afghanistan." Major Gen. John Sattler, USMC, Dir. of Operations-US CENTCOM before the House Committee on Government Reform Subcommittee on Criminal Justice, Drug Policy, and Human Resources, April 21, 2004.

[18] Lolita C. Baldor, "NATO to Provide More Afghanistan Troops," *Associated Press*, September 20, 2006.

[19] In response, Pentagon press secretary Geoff Morrell stated that, "Secretary Gates is extremely pleased that, after two days of thoughtful discussion, NATO has decided to allow ISAF forces to take on the drug traffickers who are fueling the insurgency, destabilizing Afghanistan, and killing our troops." Judy Dempsey, "NATO allows strikes on Afghan drug sites Ministers agree to major strategic shift," *International Herald Tribune*, October 11, 2008.

[20] In conjunction with the decision, ISAF released the following statement: "Based on the request of the Afghan government, consistent with the appropriate United Nations Security Council resolutions, under the existing operational plan, ISAF can act in concert with the Afghans against facilities and facilitators supporting the insurgency, in the context of counternarcotics, subject to authorization of respective nations." NATO Press Release, "NATO steps up counter-narcotics efforts in Afghanistan," October 10, 2008.

[21] Rules of engagement generally are outlined in classified documents. Author consultation with Department of Defense officials, February 2009.

[22] U.S. Department of Defense, Memorandum: Department of Defense International Counternarcotics Policy, December 24, 2008.

[23] The other combat zone with potential relevance to counternarcotics operations in Afghanistan was created January 17, 1991, in Executive Order 12744. The order designated the following areas (including air space and adjacent waters) as combat zones: Persian Gulf; Red Sea; Gulf of Oman; Gulf of Aden; that portion of the Arabian Sea that lies north of 10 degrees N. Lat., and west of 68 degrees E. Long.; and the total land areas of Iraq, Kuwait, Saudi Arabia, Oman, Bahrain, Qatar, and the United Arab Emirates.

the new U.S. military policy on counternarcotics enforcement may be being applied in Afghanistan. According to the report;

> "…two U.S. generals in Afghanistan said that the ROE and the internationally recognized Law of War have been interpreted to allow them to put drug traffickers with proven links to the insurgency on a kill list, called the joint integrated prioritized target list. The military places no restrictions on the use of force with these selected targets, which means they can be killed or captured on the battlefield; it does not, however, authorize targeted assassinations away from the battlefield. The generals said standards for getting on the list require two verifiable human sources and substantial additional evidence. Currently, there are roughly 50 major traffickers who contribute funds to the insurgency on the target list."[24]

The Defense Department has declined to comment on the specific statements included in the Senate report. However, a Pentagon spokesman said that "there is a positive, well-known connection between the drug trade and financing for the insurgency and terrorism," and, it is "important to clarify that we are targeting terrorists with links to the drug trade, rather than targeting drug traffickers with links to terrorism."[25] Thus far, U.S. and ISAF officials have declined to offer further public comment on the specific criteria currently used for targeting individuals associated with both the drug trade and insurgency.

Some observers have questioned the legal basis for the targeting of so-called "nexus targets" based on international humanitarian law (IHL), which generally prohibits the direct use of force against civilians unless and for so long as they are directly participating in hostilities.[26] Under this view, drug traffickers could be subject to direct military attack only if they are considered to be active members of the armed forces of a party to the conflict or if they are considered to be civilians directly participating in hostilities. In July 2009, the International Committee of the Red Cross (ICRC) released nonbinding interpretive guidance on the notion of direct participation in hostilities under IHL.[27] The guidance states that individuals involved with the "purchase, production, smuggling and hiding of weapons; general recruitment and training of personnel; and financial, administrative or political support to armed actors" retain the protected status against direct military attack that all civilians enjoy unless such acts qualify as "preparatory measures aiming to carry out a specific hostile act" and are "specifically designed to [inflict harm] in support of a party to an armed conflict and to the detriment of another."[28] Press reports, field surveys, and coalition military statements suggest that some individuals and groups involved in

---

[24] "Afghanistan's Narco-War: Breaking the Link Between Drug Traffickers and Insurgents," Report to the Committee on Foreign Relations, United States Senate, August 10, 2009.

[25] James Risen, "U.S. to Hunt Down Afghan Drug Lords Tied to Taliban," *New York Times*, August 10, 2009

[26] See, for example, the concerns expressed in February 2009 when purported NATO operational guidance addressing narcotics targets was leaked. Susanne Koelbl, "Battling Afghan Drug Dealers: NATO High Commander Issues Illegitimate Order to Kill," *Speigel Online*, January 28, 2009; and Matthias Gebauer and Susanne Koelbl, "Battling Drugs In Afghanistan: Order to Kill Angers German Politicians," *Speigel Online*, January 29, 2009.

[27] Available at: [http://www.icrc.org/Web/eng/siteeng0.nsf/htmlall/direct-participation-report_res/$File/direct-participation-guidance-2009-icrc.pdf].

[28] Ibid. For a discussion of the ICRC's three core criteria - threshold of harm, direct causation and belligerent nexus - see pages 46-64. According to the guidance, "Acts amounting to direct participation in hostilities must meet three cumulative requirements: (1) a threshold regarding the harm likely to result from the act, (2) a relationship of direct causation between the act and the expected harm, and (3) a belligerent nexus between the act and the hostilities conducted between the parties to an armed conflict." The guidance argues that, "In line with the distinction between direct and indirect participation in hostilities, it could be said that preparatory measures aiming to carry out a specific hostile act qualify as direct participation in hostilities, whereas preparatory measures aiming to establish the general capacity to carry out unspecified hostile acts do not."

---

narcotics trafficking provide varying levels of support to some anti-Afghan government forces, which may or may not include direct participation in hostilities on a case-by-case basis.

Expanded counternarcotics roles for the U.S. military, whether under U.S. command, or as a component of ISAF, may lead to requests for more resources. The January 2009 Defense Department report on stability and security in Afghan argued that:

> "Use of limited forces in Afghanistan is a zero-sum endeavor. A shift in force application from one mission set to another comes with a cost of a reduction of available forces for the former mission set. A shift of limited assets may result in a degradation of the [counterinsurgency] COIN mission. At the same time, the COIN mission cannot be addressed effectively without engaging in the [counternarcotics] CN mission. Additional resources, targeted to the CN mission, would be needed to expand direct DoD support to counternarcotics operations."[29]

Defense Authorization and the Provision of Equipment and Weaponry

From 2002 through 2009, Congress and the Bush Administration gradually expanded the role for U.S. military forces in training, equipping, and providing intelligence and airlift support for Afghan counternarcotics teams. To date, Defense Department authorizations for counternarcotics activities in Afghanistan have been provided via reference to Section 1033 of the Defense Authorization Act for FY1998 (P.L. 105-85, as amended) and Section 1004 of the Defense Authorization Act for FY1991 (P.L. 101-510, as amended). Both acts have been amended on a semi-annual basis to extend existing authorizations into subsequent fiscal years, to expand the authorities to include new countries, and, as written, to require reauthorization to extend beyond the end of FY2006. Since 2005, other legislative proposals to expand Defense Department counternarcotics authorities in Afghanistan have been considered, but not adopted.[30] The FY2009 Defense Authorization Act (P.L. 110-417) restated the existing authorizations and reauthorized the Secretary of Defense to provide non-lethal counternarcotics assistance to Afghanistan and a number of its neighbors (and other countries) through FY2009. The FY2010 authorization (H.R. 2647 and S. 1390) would extend the authorization through FY2010 and require the submission of an counter-drug plan for each fiscal year support is provided.

Section 1021 of the Defense Authorization Act for FY2004 (P.L. 108-136) added Afghanistan to the list of countries eligible for transfers of non-lethal Defense Department counternarcotics equipment authorized under Section 1033 of the Defense Authorization Act for FY1998 (P.L. 105-85). The FY2005 and FY2006 supplemental appropriations acts (P.L. 109-13 and P.L. 109-234) further authorized the provision of individual and crew-served weapons, ammunition, vehicles, aircraft, and detection, interception, monitoring and testing equipment to Afghan

---

[29] U.S. Department of Defense, Progress toward Security and Stability in Afghanistan. Report to Congress pursuant to Section 1230 of the 2008 National Defense Authorization Act (P.L. 110-181), January 2009, p. 99.

[30] The conference report (H.Rept. 109-360) on the Defense Authorization Act for FY2006 (P.L. 109-163) did not include a provision that was included in the Senate version of the bill (S. 1042, Section 1033) that would have authorized the Defense Department to provide a range of technical and operational support to Afghan counternarcotics authorities under Section 1004 of the Defense Authorization Act for FY1991 (P.L. 101-510). The Senate version would have authorized "the use of U.S. bases of operation or training facilities to facilitate the conduct of counterdrug activities in Afghanistan" in response to the Defense Department's request "to provide assistance in all aspects of counterdrug activities in Afghanistan, including detection, interdiction, and related criminal justice activities." (S.Rept. 109-69) This would have included transportation of personnel and supplies, maintenance and repair of equipment, the establishment and operation of bases and training facilities, and training for Afghan law enforcement personnel.

counternarcotics forces. To date, .50-caliber machine guns have been provided along with night vision equipment and a range of other supplies. Afghan counternarcotics forces have requested further weaponry in response to attacks by well armed and supplied trafficking groups. The FY2009 Defense Authorization Act (P.L. 110-417) reauthorized provision of .50-caliber and lighter crew-served weaponry and ammunition through FY2009. The FY2010 authorization (H.R. 2647 and S. 1390) would extend the authorization through FY2010.

Alternative Livelihoods and Development

As noted above, the Obama Administration has highlighted alternative livelihood and agricultural development assistance as a key component of its new strategic priorities in Afghanistan. The new Administration's focus on agriculture comes at a time when USAID alternative livelihood development programs in Afghanistan are in a period of transition, as three regional implementation programs that have been active since February 2005 are moving toward completion and are scheduled to be renewed in 2009 and 2010. As of early 2009, USAID proposals for renewed alternative livelihood programs focused on the delivery of targeted, counternarcotics-focused agricultural and development assistance to the six southern provinces where poppy cultivation has become most concentrated (Helmand, Kandahar, Zabul, Uruzgan, Nimruz, and Farah).[31] Proposals suggest that more broad-based agricultural development assistance could be extended to areas that have reduced poppy cultivation in the north, east, and west of the country. Obama Administration officials also have stated that "part of making the counternarcotics strategy more effective will be working a lot harder on crop substitution," which has been an area of congressional interest in the past.[32] According to the Obama Administration, the U.S. Department of Agriculture will "get much more involved" in Afghanistan, which may support the expansion or reorientation of USAID's alternative livelihood efforts in the agriculture sector.[33]

Eradication

Central Government and Governor-Led Eradication

The Obama Administration is "phasing out" U.S. support for poppy eradication efforts in Afghanistan in line with its strategic review and the judgment of Administration officials that eradication programs were not cost efficient and that eradication activities often proved counterproductive. The policy change comes after years of debate in Washington, DC, Kabul, and across Europe about the relative merits and drawbacks of supporting Afghan government poppy eradication efforts.

Proponents of forced eradication have long argued that destroying large portions of Afghanistan's opium poppy crops is necessary in order to establish and maintain a credible deterrent for farmers

---

[31] Author consultation with USAID Afghanistan Desk, February 2009.

[32] Remarks By Undersecretary of Defense for Policy Michele Flournoy, Brookings Institution, Washington, D.C., Federal News Service, March 27, 2009. The House report on H.R. 2765 (H.Rept. 110-197) directed the Secretary of State to initiate a pilot crop substitution program in "an area in which poppy production is prevalent."

[33] Comments of Bruce Reidel, The White House, Office of the Press Secretary, Press Briefing by Bruce Riedel, Ambassador Richard Holbrooke, and Michelle Flournoy on the New Strategy for Afghanistan and Pakistan, March 27, 2009.

and landowners in line with Afghan law. Critics of forced eradication argued in response that eradication in the absence of existing alternative livelihood options for Afghan farmers contributes to the likelihood that farmers will continue to cultivate opium poppy in the future and may encourage some farmers and landowners to support anti-government elements, including the Taliban.

To date, U.S. and Afghan authorities have maintained that the Central Poppy Eradication Force and governor-led eradication programs have been effective in deterring and reducing some opium poppy cultivation. However, given recurrent clashes between eradication forces and farmers and accounts of selective, politicized eradication efforts by local authorities, other observers and officials have expressed concern about the safety and effectiveness of current ground-based eradication efforts. The Bush Administration sought to improve eradication results by embedding "poppy elimination" teams in key opium poppy growing provinces to monitor and advise on early season, locally-executed eradication activities. The strategy was designed to minimize violent farmer resistance to central government forces and give farming families time to plant replacement cash crops. At present, it remains unclear how the Obama Administration's decision to "phase out" U.S. support to eradication efforts will affect the Afghan government's commitment to continue its eradication efforts or the effectiveness of those efforts.

Manual or Aerial Herbicide-based Eradication

Afghan and U.S. authorities discussed the introduction of aerial herbicide-based eradication to Afghanistan in late 2004, but decided against initiating a program in early 2005 due to financial, logistical, and political considerations. Since 2006, ground-based eradication results have varied drastically based on location and local political and security conditions. This has led some to renew their calls for the introduction of stronger eradication methods, including the use of herbicides to kill poppy plants. With the Obama Administration's policy changes in place, the prospects for such a program look increasingly unlikely. Nevertheless, policy makers and Members of Congress may engage in further debate concerning options for using herbicides for manual or aerial poppy eradication and their possible risks and rewards.

In the past, Afghan President Hamid Karzai has expressed categorical opposition to the use of aerial eradication, citing public health and environmental safety concerns.[34] The 2006 Afghan national drug control strategy also stated that the Afghan government "has also decided that eradication must only be delivered by manual or mechanical ground based means."[35] Bush Administration officials argued for more widespread and non-negotiated eradication operations and stated that while herbicides may be efficient and safe, U.S. officials would follow the decisions of Afghan officials concerning their potential use. Since FY2005, Congress has sought to prohibit or condition the use of appropriated funds to support aerial herbicide spraying in Afghanistan. In the 111th Congress, the Omnibus Appropriations Act, 2009 (H.R. 1105; P.L. 111-8) specifies that:

---

[34] Office of the Spokesperson to the President—Transitional Islamic State of Afghanistan. "About the Commitment by the Government of Afghanistan to the Fight Against Narcotics and Concerns About the Aerial Spraying of Poppy Fields." In January 2007, President Karzai announced that any herbicide-based eradication efforts would be delayed, and presidential spokesmen have since repeated their criticism of herbicides on numerous occasions. It appears unlikely that President Karzai would approve a controversial measure such as aerial eradication in the run up to the presidential election scheduled for August 2009.

[35] Afghanistan Ministry of Counternarcotics, Updated NDCS, January 2006, p. 21.

"none of the funds appropriated under this heading for assistance for Afghanistan may be made available for eradication programs through the aerial spraying of herbicides unless the Secretary of State determines and reports to the Committees on Appropriations that the President of Afghanistan has requested assistance for such aerial spraying programs for counternarcotics or counterterrorism purposes."

The Act further requires the Secretary of State to consult with the Committees on Appropriations prior to the obligation of funds for an aerial eradication programs in the event that such a determination is made.

Counternarcotics Assistance Certification and Reporting Requirements

Since 2002, funding for U.S. counternarcotics operations in Afghanistan has consisted of U.S. program costs and financial and material assistance to Afghan counternarcotics organizations. Although poppy cultivation and drug trafficking were widespread prior to the fall of the Taliban regime, U.S. counternarcotics programs in the region were limited, and focused on eliminating poppy cultivation and supporting interdiction activities in neighboring countries. U.S. funding for counternarcotics programs in Afghanistan did not increase dramatically until FY2005, when the Bush Administration submitted requests to Congress for funding to support the introduction of the five pillar counternarcotics strategy (See **Table 2** above, and "U.S. Policy Initiatives: Transition from the "Five-Pillar" Plan" below).

Certification Requirements

Since 2006, Congress has placed conditions on some amounts of U.S. economic assistance to Afghanistan by requiring the President to certify that the Afghan government is cooperating fully with counternarcotics efforts prior to the obligation of funds or to issue a national security waiver. The conditions serve as signal of congressional views that U.S. assistance should not be given to a government not fully cooperating with U.S. counternarcotics efforts unless U.S. national security would be jeopardized if assistance were withheld. The 2006 Foreign Operations Appropriations Act (P.L. 109-102) stated that no more than $225 in Economic Support Fund (ESF) assistance could be obligated until the President certified to Congress that the Afghan government "at both the national and local level is cooperating fully with United States funded poppy eradication and interdiction efforts." The Act provided waiver authority to the President if he deemed it necessary to preserve the vital national security interests of the United States. The Bush Administration issued a waiver of the certification requirement for FY2006 ESF appropriations for Afghanistan on May 22, 2006.[36]

Subsequent appropriations legislation also has included these provisions. For FY2007, the FY2006 conditions were carried forward based on the provisions of the Revised Continuing Appropriations Resolution, 2007 (P.L. 110-5).[37] The certification and justification report were

---

[36] U.S. Department of State Public Notice 5486, "Determination To Waive the Certification Requirement that the Government of Afghanistan Is Cooperating Fully with U.S.-Funded Poppy Eradication and Interdiction Efforts in Afghanistan," May 22, 2006. *Federal Register*, Volume 71, Number 153, August 9, 2006.

[37] The House version of the FY2007 Foreign Operations Appropriations Act (H.R. 5522) would have limited the obligation of Economic Support Fund (ESF) assistance to Afghanistan to $225 million until the Secretary of State certified to the Appropriations committees that the Afghan government "at both the national and local level" was fully (continued...)

completed in June 2007. The FY2008 Consolidated Appropriations Act (P.L. 110-161, H.R. 2764) limited the obligation of FY2008 ESF assistance to Afghanistan to $300 million until the Secretary of State certified to the Appropriations committees that the Afghan government "at both the national and local level" was fully cooperating with U.S.-funded poppy eradication and drug interdiction efforts. The Act provided for a presidential waiver of this provision, subject to a reporting requirement. The Bush Administration waived the certification requirement for FY2008 ESF appropriations for Afghanistan on May 9, 2008 and issued a detailed report to Congress justifying its decision and describing U.S. and Afghan counternarcotics efforts and remaining challenges.[38]

In the 111th Congress, the Omnibus Appropriations Act, 2009, states that $200,000,000 in ESF funding may be obligated "only after the Secretary of State certifies to the Committees on Appropriations that the Government of Afghanistan at both the national and provincial level is cooperating fully with United States-funded poppy eradication and interdiction efforts in Afghanistan." The Act provides for a presidential waiver based on national security determination. The House version of the FY2010 Foreign Operations Appropriations bill (H.R. 3081) states that $300,000,000 in ESF funding may be obligated "only after the Secretary of State certifies to the Committees on Appropriations that the Government of Afghanistan at both the national and provincial level is cooperating fully with United States-funded poppy eradication and interdiction efforts in Afghanistan." The Act provides for a presidential waiver based on national security determination. The Senate version of the bill (S. 1434) states that $55 million in International Narcotics Control and Law Enforcement (INCLE) funds for Afghanistan may not be obligated "unless the Secretary of State certifies to the Committees on Appropriations that the Government of Afghanistan is cooperating fully with United States efforts against the Taliban and Al Qaeda and to reduce poppy cultivation and illicit drug trafficking." The Senate version provides for a waiver authority based on a national security interests determination.

Reporting Requirements

Since 2002, Congress has required the executive branch to submit a number of detailed reports on its counternarcotics strategies and the use of appropriated funds to support counternarcotics programs in Afghanistan. Among these reports are worldwide annual surveys of Defense Department counterdrug activities, required reports justifying the waiver of conditions on U.S. ESF assistance, and specific reports on the opiate trade in and around Afghanistan and Administration plans to combat it. The following list highlights a number of recent reports that may be of interest to Congress for oversight purposes. It is not exhaustive:

- Section 7104 of the Intelligence Reform and Terrorism Prevention Act of 2004 (P.L. 108-458) required the submission of an interagency report that described current progress toward the reduction of poppy cultivation and heroin production in Afghanistan and provided detail on the extent to which drug profits support

---

(...continued)

cooperating with U.S.-funded poppy eradication and drug interdiction efforts. The Senate version of the FY2007 foreign operations bill did not contain this provision.

[38] U.S. Department of State, *Justification for the Waiver and the Status of Cooperation by the Government of Afghanistan with the United States Funded Poppy Eradication and Interdiction Efforts in Afghanistan*, April 2008, transmitted to Congress May 12, 2008.

terrorist groups and anti-government elements in and around Afghanistan. The report was completed in October 2005.[39]

- P.L. 110-28 required the DEA Administrator to submit a report by July 31, 2007 that included a plan to target and arrest Afghan drug kingpins in Helmand and Kandahar provinces.

- House report on H.R. 2764 (H.Rept. 110-197) required the Administration to report on "the use of aerial assets to include fixed and rotary wing aircraft in coordination with and in support of Drug Enforcement Administration (DEA) counternarcotics operations," and, "the extradition status of Afghan drug kingpins and narco terrorists, the destruction of Afghan heroin laboratories, local Afghan prosecutions of heroin-related crimes, and illegal border crossings by foreign nationals from Pakistan into Afghanistan."

- The National Defense Authorization Act, 2008 (Section 1230, P.L. 110-181) requires the executive branch to submit a report on the comprehensive strategy of the United States for security and stability in Afghanistan every 180 days through FY2010. The reports issued to date have included sections devoted to counternarcotics policy as well as other issues such as police training and judicial reform relevant to U.S. and Afghan counternarcotics goals.

- The FY2009 Defense Authorization Act (P.L. 110-417) extended the requirement for annual Defense Department reporting on its overseas counterdrug activities through 2009, and Section 1026 of the Act requires the Secretary of Defense to submit by June 30, 2009, "a comprehensive strategy of the Department of the Defense with regard to counter-narcotics efforts in the South and Central Asian regions, including the countries of Afghanistan, Turkmenistan, Tajikistan, Kyrgyzstan, Kazakhstan, Pakistan, and India, as well as the countries of Armenia, Azerbaijan, and China."

Background

During the more than two decades of occupation, foreign interference, and civil war that followed the 1979 Soviet invasion, opium poppy cultivation and drug trafficking were essential components of Afghanistan's war economy, providing revenue to individuals and groups competing for power and an economic survival mechanism to a growing segment of the impoverished population. In December 2001, Afghan leaders participating in the Bonn conference that formed Afghanistan's interim post-Taliban government echoed pleas issued by their pro-Communist predecessors decades earlier:[40] They strongly urged that "the United Nations, the international community, and regional organizations cooperate with the Interim Authority to combat international terrorism, cultivation, and trafficking of illicit drugs and provide Afghan farmers with financial, material and technical resources for alternative crop

---

[39] Report on Counter Drug Efforts in Afghanistan—October 18, 2005, as required by Sec. 7104, Section 207 (b) of the Intelligence Reform and Terrorism Prevention Act, 2004 (P.L. 108-458); House Committee on International Relations, Ex. Comm. 4575.

[40] In 1978, pro-Communist Afghan officials reportedly requested "a lot of assistance from abroad, especially economic help, to help replace farmers' incomes derived from opium poppy cultivation." Randal, *Washington Post*, November 2, 1978.

production."[41] In spite of renewed efforts on the part of Afghan and international authorities to combat opium poppy cultivation since the fall of the Taliban, Afghanistan remains the world's leading producer of opium.

Opium and Afghanistan's War Economy

Following the Soviet invasion of 1979 and during the civil war that ensued in the aftermath of the Soviet withdrawal, opium poppy cultivation expanded in parallel with the gradual collapse of state authority across Afghanistan. As the country's formal economy succumbed to violence and disorder, opium became one of the few available commodities capable of both storing economic value and generating revenue for local administration and military supplies. Some anti-Soviet mujahedeen commanders encouraged and taxed opium poppy cultivation and drug shipments, and, in some instances, participated in the narcotics trade directly as a means of both economic survival and military financing.[42] Elements of Pakistan's Inter-Services Intelligence (ISI) agency and Afghan rebel commanders to which the ISI channeled U.S. funding and weaponry are also alleged to have participated in the Afghan narcotics trade during the Soviet occupation and its aftermath, including in the production and trafficking of refined heroin to U.S. and European markets.[43] After the withdrawal of Soviet troops and a drop in U.S. and Soviet funding, opium poppy cultivation, drug trafficking, and other criminal activities increasingly provided local leaders and military commanders with a means of supporting their operations and establishing political influence in the areas they controlled.

Taliban Era

The centralization of authority under the Taliban movement during the mid-to-late 1990s further fueled Afghan opium poppy cultivation and narcotic production, as Taliban officials co-opted their military opponents with promises of permissive cultivation policies and mirrored the practices of their warlord predecessors by collecting tax revenue and profits on the growing output.[44] In 1999, Afghanistan produced a then-all time high of over 4500 MT of raw opium, which led to growing international pressure from governments whose citizens were consuming the end products of a seemingly endless supply of Afghan drugs. In response, the Taliban announced a ban on opium poppy cultivation in late 2000, but allowed the opiate trade to continue, fueling speculation that the decision was designed to contribute to their marginalized government's campaign for international legitimacy.

---

[41] Agreement on Provisional Arrangements in Afghanistan Pending the Re-establishment of Permanent Government Institutions [The Bonn Agreement], December 5, 2001.

[42] See Arthur Bonner, "Afghan Rebel's Victory Garden: Opium," *New York Times*, June 18, 1986, and Mary Thornton, "Sales of Opium Reportedly Fund Afghan Rebels," *Washington Post*, December 17, 1983.

[43] See James Rupert and Steve Coll, "U.S. Declines to Probe Afghan Drug Trade: Rebels, Pakistani Officers Implicated," *Washington Post*, May 13, 1990; Jim Lobe, "Drugs: U.S. Looks Other Way In Afghanistan and Pakistan," *Inter Press Service*, May 18, 1990; John F. Burns, "U.S. Cuts Off Arms to Afghan Faction," *New York Times*, November 19, 1989; Kathy Evans, "Money is the Drug," *The Guardian* (UK), November 11, 1989; and Lawrence Lifschultz, "Bush, Drugs and Pakistan: Inside the Kingdom of Heroin," *The Nation*, November 14, 1988.

[44] The Taliban government collected an agricultural tax (approximately 10%, paid in kind), known as *ushr*, and a traditional Islamic tithe known as *zakat* (variable percentages). The Taliban also taxed opium traders and transport syndicates involved in the transportation of opiates. UNODC, "The Opium Economy in Afghanistan," pp. 92, 127-8.

Under the ban, opium poppy cultivation was reduced dramatically and overall opium output fell to 185 MT, mainly because of continued cultivation and production in areas under the control of Northern Alliance forces. Individual Northern Alliance commanders also taxed opium production and transportation within their zones of control and continued producing opium and trafficking heroin following the Taliban prohibition.[45] Although U.S. and international officials initially applauded the Taliban policy shift, many experts now believe that the ban was designed to increase the market price for and potential revenue from stocks of Afghan opium maintained by the Taliban and its powerful trafficking allies within the country.[46]

Post-Taliban Resurgence

Following 9/11, Afghan farmers anticipated the fall of the Taliban government and resumed cultivating opium poppy as U.S.-led military operations began in October 2001. International efforts to rebuild Afghanistan's devastated society began with the organization of an interim administration at the Bonn Conference in December 2001, and Afghan leaders committed their new government to combat the resurgence of opium poppy cultivation and requested international counternarcotics assistance from the United States, the United Kingdom and others.[47] The United Kingdom was designated the lead nation for international counternarcotics assistance and policy in Afghanistan. On January 17, 2002, the Afghan Interim Administration issued a ban on opium poppy cultivation that was enforced with a limited eradication campaign in April 2002. In spite of these efforts, the 2001-2002 opium poppy crop produced over 3400 MT of opium, reestablishing Afghanistan as the world's leading producer of illicit opium.

Since 2002, further government bans and stronger interdiction and eradication efforts have failed to overcome vastly increased opium poppy cultivation and opium output, although year-to-year reductions in nationwide estimates occurred from 2004 to 2005 and again from 2007 to 2008. Increasingly, U.S. policymakers and military commanders have focused on apparent financial linkages between the drug trade and a range of anti-U.S. and anti-Afghan government groups, including Taliban insurgents. One January 2009 press account cited an unnamed U.S. military officer describing the current dynamic in southern Afghanistan as follows: "Drugs out, guns in."[48] Recent history suggests that this dynamic is consistent rather than new: since the Soviet invasion period, various non-state actors in Afghanistan and surrounding countries have used the drug trade as a means of financing their activities, particularly in areas where insecurity or corruption have allowed poppy cultivation and drug trafficking to thrive.

---

[45] UNODC, "The Opium Economy in Afghanistan," p. 92.

[46] In December 2001, then Assistant Secretary of State for International Narcotics and Law Enforcement Affairs Rand Beers stated that the Taliban had not banned opium cultivation "out of kindness, but because they wanted to regulate the market: They simply produced too much opium." Marc Kaufman, "Surge in Afghan Poppy Crop Is Forecast," *Washington Post*, December 25, 2001. See **Table 1** and UNODC, Opium Economy in Afghanistan, p. 57.

[47] The Bonn Agreement, December 5, 2001.

[48] Dexter Filkins, "Taliban Fill NATO's Big Gaps in Afghan South," *New York Times*, January 21, 2009.

Actors in Afghanistan's Opium Economy

Ongoing field research indicates that the motives and methods of drug trade participants vary considerably based on their location, their respective economic circumstances, their relationships with local and external groups, and prevailing political and security conditions.[49] While basic profit incentives motivate many actors, significant differences in cultivation patterns from district to district and changes in district cultivation patterns over time suggest that a broader range of variables influence the decisions of farmers, landowners, laborers, traffickers, officials, and insurgents. These variables include market prices of opium and licit crops, the availability and cost of agricultural inputs, weather, and government enforcement activities. As a result, many experts and practitioners believe that counternarcotics strategies should employ a mix of policy tools adapted to varying local conditions in order to achieve sustainable results. This includes measures to reduce the global demand for illicit opiates, which ultimately drives the narcotics trade in Afghanistan and in other countries (see "Trafficking and Consumption Markets").

Farmers

According to the U.S. Central Intelligence Agency, an estimated 80% of Afghans are employed in the agriculture sector, and non-opium agriculture accounts for 31% of Afghanistan's GDP. Since 2001, high opium prices, insecurity, and corruption have encouraged and enabled the spread of poppy farming beyond areas where it previously had been concentrated. Profit motives and economic opportunism have led many new farmers into the opium market during this period, while many others have continued or have begun using opium poppy cultivation as an income security strategy alongside other crops. Field research suggests that opium has continuously served as a substitute source of income and a store of value for some Afghans during successive periods of conflict, drought, and economic disruption.

Field studies have identified several factors that affect the profitability of opium poppy and legal crops for Afghan farmers. As in other markets, the extent and terms of Afghan farmers' access to land, water, agricultural supplies, and credit directly affect the production costs of both legal and illicit crops. In areas of Afghanistan where land ownership and water rights are highly centralized or key agricultural supplies remain scarce, some farmers sell crops at rates below market value in exchange for access to needed inputs. Landless farmers often seek sharecropping arrangements with landowners who control access to land and water and may dictate crop selection. In all cases, severe and variable weather patterns can drastically affect output.

Household debt levels and credit requirements also influence cultivation preferences among Afghan farmers.[50] An informal crop-for-credit system, known as *salaam*, has long allowed farmers to secure loans for inputs or winter supplies based on agreements to sell harvested crops

---

[49] Analysis in this report relating to the motives and methods of various participants in Afghanistan's narcotics trade is based on a broad survey of available field research gathered over a fifteen year period. Key sources include the UNODC's "Strategic Studies" series on Afghanistan's opium economy and a series of analytical reports prepared for the government of the United Kingdom, the World Bank, the Aga Khan Foundation, and the Afghanistan Research and Evaluation Unit by field researchers David Mansfield, Adam Pain, William Byrd, Frank Kenefick, Larry Morgan, and others. For a complete list of studies consulted see "Cited Field Surveys and Research Studies" on page 48 .

[50] Adam Pain, "Opium Poppy and Informal Credit," Afghanistan Research and Evaluation Unit Issues Paper Series, October 2008.

---

at contracted rates. For both licit and illicit crops, weather-induced crop failures have the potential to compound informal debts by destroying output that serves as collateral and payment. Fluctuating commodity prices also create substantial risks for *salaam* borrowers and lenders. This is doubly true for opium, which is subject to eradication and wide fluctuations in market prices based on security conditions. Some field reporting suggests that increases in household debt due to weather, eradication, and changing prices have compelled farmers in various regions to mortgage land or expand poppy cultivation as an economic coping strategy. Other research indicates that poppy cultivation has allowed some Afghans to repay debt obligations accumulated during previous periods of drought and conflict. The Afghan government issued a decree banning opium-based loans and credit in April 2002, and recent surveys suggest that opium-based lending has declined as credit availability has increased and opium prices have fallen as stockpiles have grown since 2001 (see **Table 1**).

Land Owners and Laborers

Land owners who control vital opium poppy cultivation inputs like land, water, and fertilizers enjoy an economic advantage in the opium production cycle, which places heavy demands on Afghanistan's rural agricultural labor market during annual opium poppy planting, maintenance, and harvesting seasons. Although opium prices have fallen since reaching a peak of $350/kg in 2002, UNODC reports suggest that landless farmers have experienced greater profit loss than land owners.[53] Some land owners and creditors have benefitted from consolidation of property related to credit needs and debt obligations of some Afghan farmers. Some land owners secure the services of skilled itinerant laborers to assist in the complex opium harvesting process, which improves crop yields and revenue. In turn, itinerant laborers have contributed to the spread of poppy cultivation and opium harvesting expertise across Afghanistan.[54]

Corrupt Officials and Militia

According to the U.S. State Department's 2009 International Narcotics Control Strategy Report (INCSR) on Afghanistan, "many Afghan government officials are believed to profit from the drug trade," and "narcotics-related corruption is particularly pervasive at the provincial and district levels of government."[55] In the past, Afghan counternarcotics officials have stated that "high government officials, police commanders, governors are involved" in the drug trade and have identified "former commanders and warlords who are still in power" serving as "district chiefs and local police" as the main problem with regard to corruption.[56]

Corruption Allegations: Police, Governors, and Legislators

The U.S. State Department's 2009 International Narcotics Control Strategy Report (INCSR) on Afghanistan notes the 2008 conviction of nine public officials, including Kabul police commanders, on heroin trafficking charges. The Afghan National Police commander of Takhar Province also was removed from office, but his associates, who had been convicted on drug related charges were pardoned in April 2009 by President Karzai. High-level government appointees also have been alleged to be involved in narcotics trafficking. The former governor of Helmand province, Sher Mohammed Akhundzada, was removed from office after 9 metric tons of opium were found at his offices in June 2005.[51] Karzai and Akhundzada reportedly have been close friends since the 1980s. When asked about the case later that year, President Karzai said, "We don't need to have an investigation on [Sher Mohammed]. We will remove him from his place and bring him to do some other government work. Maybe he should become a senator or something."[52] President Karzai appointed Akhundzada to Afghanistan's House of Elders (Senate equivalent) in December 2005. In June 2006, Akhundzada remains the subject of debate between some Afghan and coalition authorities. Some Afghan officials argue his dismissal as governor led to increased insecurity in Helmand, while some coalition members reportedly suspect Akhundzada's allies in southern Afghanistan of continuing involvement in the drug trade.

---

[51] John Jennings, "Opium Crops Flourish in Afghanistan after U.S. Breaks Aid Promise," *Reuters*, July 4, 1991; Paul Watson, "Where Taliban Rules Again," *Los Angeles Times*, June 24, 2006; and, DEA Administrator Karen P. Tandy Statement Before the House Committee on Armed Services, June 28, 2006.

[52] Steve Kroft, "Afghanistan: Addicted to Heroin," *60 Minutes* (CBS), October 16, 2005.

[53] UNODC, "Afghanistan Opium Survey 2003," p. 8.

[54] See UNODC, "An Analysis of the Process of Expansion of Opium Poppy Cultivation to New Districts in Afghanistan," June 1998.

[55] Available at: http://www.state.gov/p/inl/rls/nrcrpt/2009/vol1/116520.htm.

[56] "Curbing Rampant Afghan Opium Trade Will Take Karzai Years," *Agence France-Presse*, December 5, 2004; and Pamela Constable, "A Poor Yield For Afghans' War on Drugs," *Washington Post*, September 19, 2006.

Most of Afghanistan's prominent political figures have publicly condemned the country's opium economy. However, some political figures and their powerful supporters are alleged to have links with the trade or maintain influence over areas of Afghanistan where opium poppy cultivation and drug trafficking take place. U.S. Ambassador Thomas Schweich, who resigned in mid-2008 as the U.S. Coordinator for Counternarcotics and Justice Reform in Afghanistan, wrote in July 2008 that "while it is true that [President] Karzai's Taliban enemies finance themselves from the drug trade, so do many of his supporters."[57] Press reports in October 2008 renewed allegations that Ahmed Wali Karzai, President Karzai's brother, has been involved with narcotics trafficking.[58] The president and his brother strongly denied the allegations.

The 2009 INCSR states that "in many provinces, opium markets exist under the control of regional warlords who also control the illicit arms trade and other criminal activities, including trafficking in persons." In some cases, commanders, warlords, and militia under the control of former cabinet members, former presidential candidates, and members of parliament also have been alleged to participate in the opium trade.[59] Government authorities and security forces in Afghanistan have accused each other of involvement in opium production and trafficking, and militia commanders have clashed over opium production and profits in various regions of the country, threatening the country's stability and the lives of civilians.[60] With regard to the Afghan parliament, some experts have argued that drug money may have financed the campaigns of candidates in 2004, and at least one expert warned that "drug lords" were candidates.[61]

As the Afghan government develops stronger counternarcotics policies and capabilities, groups that are involved with the opium trade may join others in seeking to disrupt security and corrupt or subvert Afghanistan's democratic process. While the 2006 INCSR report warned that President Karzai's "ability to move vigorously against corruption... is severely constrained by the practical political considerations of a nascent central government," subsequent INCSRs and press reports have detailed a number of steps taken by the Afghan government to implement anti-corruption measures. These measures have grown in scope, although U.S. government reports in mid-2008 concluded that counternarcotics operations remained "severely constrained by the capacity of the Afghan law enforcement and judicial system."[62] As capacity improves, political will becomes a more important determining factor.

---

[57] Thomas Schweich, "Is Afghanistan a Narco-State?" *New York Times Magazine*, July 27, 2008.

[58] James Risen and Carlotta Gall, "Reports Link Karzai's Brother to Afghanistan Heroin Trade," *New York Times*, October 5, 2008.

[59] See Victoria Burnett, "Outlook Uncertain: Can Afghanistan Take the Next Step to Building a State?" *Financial Times*, August 19, 2004; Carol Harrington, "Ruthless Dostum a Rival for Karzai," *Toronto Star*, September 20, 2004; and Jurgen Dahlkamp, Susanne Koelbl, and Georg Mascolo, (tr. Margot Bettauer Dembo), "Bundeswehr: Poppies, Rocks, Shards of Trouble," *Der Spiegel* [Germany], November 10, 2003.

[60] See "7 Are Killed in a Clash of Afghan Militias," *New York Times*, February 9, 2004.

[61] Anne Barnard and Farah Stockman, "U.S. Weighs Role in Heroin War in Afghanistan," *Boston Globe*, October 20, 2004.

[62] U.S. Department of Defense, *Report on Progress toward Security and Stability in Afghanistan*, June 2008, p. 67. Report to Congress in accordance with the 2008 National Defense Authorization Act (Section 1230, P.L. 110-181).

Traffickers and Criminal Syndicates

According to the United Nations Office on Drugs and Crime (UNODC), the global dynamics of the illicit opiates market "are not well understood."[63] Publicly available information and statistics on the production of illicit opiates, their relative value, and the behavior of international opiate traffickers and markets are often derived from limited survey and international police seizure reporting data. The UNODC produces data on international trafficking of illicit Afghan opiates based in part on reports of the seizure of various opiates by security forces in Afghanistan and surrounding countries.[64]

According to UNODC, 50% of Afghan opiates are trafficked via Iran, while 35% are trafficked via Pakistan and approximately 15% are trafficked into Central Asia. Production and trafficking patterns for refined opiates vary by region in Afghanistan.[65] UNODC argued in its 2008 World Drug Report that the shift of opium poppy cultivation toward southern Afghanistan has caused a corresponding decrease in the amount of opiates trafficked along the so-called Northern or Silk Route through Central Asia in favor of the so-called Balkan and Black Sea routes through Iran, Pakistan, Turkey, and the Balkan states. Trafficking by air to Asian and African destinations remains a low-level but persistent challenge.

Although Afghan individuals and groups play a significant role in trafficking opiates within Afghanistan and into surrounding countries, relatively few Afghans have been identified as participants in the international narcotics trafficking operations that transport and distribute finished opiate products such as heroin to Asian, Middle Eastern, European, African, or North American consumer markets.[66] Ethnic and tribal relationships facilitate the opium trade within Afghanistan, while relationships between ethnic Tajik, Uzbek, Pashtun, and Baluch Afghans and their counterparts in Central Asia, Pakistan, and Iran provide a basis for the organization and networking needed to deliver Afghan opiates to regional markets and into the hands of international trafficking organizations.

International market prices for heroin and intermediate opiates such as morphine ensure that individuals and groups engaged in the shipment and distribution of refined opium products earn substantially higher profits than those involved with cultivating and producing raw opium gum.[67] The 2008 UNODC Afghanistan Opium Survey indicated that the average price of heroin in border regions of countries neighboring Afghanistan was $3,284/kg in 2008. The comparable average price for opium was $464/kg. According to the UNODC, approximately 60% of the

---

[63] United Nations Office on Drugs and Crime (UNODC), World Drug Report 2007, p. 37.

[64] Detailed information about UNODC methodology can be found in the following report: UNODC, The Opium Economy in Afghanistan – An International Problem, 2003.

[65] According to the UNODC, "there are important opium markets and heroin laboratories in the Musa Qala and Sangin districts of Helmand [province]. However, these laboratories and markets have so far not been destroyed. In the southern and eastern parts of Afghanistan, opiate and precursor trafficking is mainly controlled by tribes whereas in the northern provinces they are controlled by local commanders." UNODC, Afghanistan Opium Survey, 2007.

[66] According to the UNODC, "the involvement of Afghan groups/individuals is basically limited to the opium production, the trade of opium within Afghanistan, the transformation of some of the opium into morphine and heroin, and to some extent, the trafficking of opiates to neighboring countries." UNODC, The Opium Economy in Afghanistan, p. 64. However, the UNODC also has reported that "some Afghan traffickers do not only ship the opium or heroin to the borders of neighboring countries, but also onwards to major transshipment places where prices are usually far higher." UNODC, Afghanistan Opium Survey, 2004, p.110.

[67] See UNODC, "The Opium Economy in Afghanistan," pp. 129-40, 165-8.

---

opium produced in Afghanistan is converted to heroin or morphine within the country, and the rest is exported in raw form.[68]

The opium-to-heroin conversion process requires the use of so-called "precursor chemicals," such as acetic anhydride, that are not produced in Afghanistan. As such, monitoring agencies, including UNODC and the U.S. Drug Enforcement Administration (DEA), devote resources to controlling the inflow of precursors. Authorities in Afghanistan and other countries announced a number of large acetic anhydride seizures in 2007 and 2008, including the seizures of 10 tons in Russia, five tons in Bandar Abbas, Iran, and 14 tons in Karachi, Pakistan. In June 2008, the United Nations Security Council unanimously adopted Resolution 1817, which calls on all U.N. member states "to increase international and regional cooperation in order to counter the illicit production and trafficking of drugs in Afghanistan, including by strengthening the monitoring of the international trade in chemical precursors."

Although opium refining facilities that produce morphine base and heroin traditionally have been located in tribal areas along the Afghan border with Pakistan, the growth and spread of opium cultivation in recent years has led to a corresponding proliferation of opiate processing facilities. The large proportion of heroin in the composition of drugs seized in countries neighboring Afghanistan reflects this proliferation and suggests that the profitability of opiate trafficking for Afghan groups is likely to have increased significantly since 2001. In 2002, the UNODC estimated the annual turn-over in the international trade in Afghan opiates to be $30 billion.[69] Some observers argue that trafficking profits have a greater potential to fuel economic and political instability and that interdiction and prosecution of high level traffickers should precede eradication efforts that may drive up raw opium prices. Multilateral interdiction operations have been ongoing since 2001 (see "Interdiction" below).

Taliban and Insurgent Groups

Afghan, U.S., and coalition officials believe that linkages between insurgents, terrorists, and narcotics traffickers threaten the security of Afghanistan and the international community. Although much of the conflict between regional and factional militias that once fueled opium cultivation in Afghanistan has now ended, long-established political and commercial networks linking armed groups, landowning elites, transportation guilds, and drug syndicates continue to constitute the foundation of the opium economy. In addition to moving opiates, sophisticated drug transportation and money laundering networks reportedly facilitate the movement of individuals, funds, and weapons for the Taliban, Al Qaeda, and other insurgent groups. In return, Taliban fighters and others provide protection for narcotics activity reportedly including cultivation and shipments. In the past, British officials have warned of "alliances of convenience" based on the use of drug money to recruit tribal "foot soldiers" for insurgent activities.[70]

Anecdotal reporting suggests that armed and well-financed trafficking groups may be encouraging Afghan farmers and employing insurgents to violently resist drug interdiction and poppy eradication efforts. Since 2003, poppy eradication teams employed by provincial or

---

[68] UNODC/MCN, Afghanistan Opium Survey 2008, p. 127.

[69] UNODC, Afghanistan Opium Survey, 2002, p. 5.

[70] United Kingdom Defense Secretary Des Browne, "Speech to the Royal United Services Institute," London, September 19, 2006.

national authorities consistently have faced demonstrations, small arms fire, mined poppy fields, and attacks by RPGs and mortars.[71] Some clashes have involved eradication teams with U.S. participants and official advisers.[72] In order to better respond to the threat of organized violent resistance to eradication and interdiction operations, the U.S. military is working with the Afghan Ministry of Defense to create a military unit dedicated to providing perimeter security for counternarcotics operations (see "Institutions and Forces" below).

Narcotics Trafficking and the Taliban: Recent U.S. Indictments

U.S. officials have indicted three prominent figures alleged to have been involved in Afghanistan's drug trade and alleged to have financed or otherwise supported the Taliban. Two of these figures reportedly had been detained previously by U.S. forces and may have provided intelligence and security assistance to U.S. military operations.

Haji Bashir Noorzai is a Pashtun clan leader alleged to have been a "major financial supporter of the Taliban"[73] and was arrested in New York in April 2005 and charged with conspiracy to import heroin into the United States over a 15-year period. He reportedly agreed to travel to the United States in order to provide intelligence that would assist coalition efforts to stabilize southern Afghanistan.[74] Press accounts state that Noorzai voluntarily provided intelligence about the Taliban during questioning at Kandahar airport in 2002 and reportedly later turned in weapons and provided security support to local officials.[75] The indictment charged that Noorzai and his organization "provided demolitions, weaponry, and manpower to the Taliban" in return for "protection for its opium crops, heroin laboratories, drug-transportation routes, and members and associates."[76] He was convicted in April 2009 and sentenced to life in prison.

Haji Baz Mohammed was convicted in October 2007 for importing Afghan heroin into the United States as the leader of a drug organization in the eastern province of Nangarhar. He was extradited to the United States in October 2005 to face charges. According to his indictment, Mohammed's organization was "closely aligned with the Taliban" and "provided financial support to the Taliban and other associated Islamic-extremist organizations in Afghanistan" in return for protection.[77] He pled guilty in 2006 and was sentenced to more than 15 years in prison.

Haji Juma Khan is an alleged drug organization leader and Taliban financier. He reportedly was detained in Indonesia after arriving from Dubai and turned over to U.S. authorities. According to his indictment, Khan allegedly "was closely aligned with the Taliban" and he and his organization allegedly "provided financial support to the Taliban, in the form of the Khan Organization's drug trafficking activities, in exchange for protection for the organization's drug trafficking operations."[78]

---

[71] The Afghan government's Central Eradication Force reportedly was "rocketed by furious villagers" during a 2004 eradication mission in Wardak province outside of Kabul. *Reuters*, Pressure on Karzai as Afghan Drug Problem Worsens, October 5, 2004.

[72] Jon Lee Anderson, "The Taliban's Opium War," *New Yorker*, Vol. 83:19, July 9, 2007.

[73] Liz Sly, "Opium Cash Fuels Terror, Experts Say," *Chicago Tribune*, February 9, 2004; John Fullerton, "Live and Let Live for Afghan Warlords, Drug Barons," *Reuters*, February 5, 2002.

[74] Bill Powell "Warlord or Druglord?" Time Magazine, February 8, 2007; Benjamin Weiser, "Facing Drug Trial, Afghan Says He Aided U.S.", New York Times, September 9, 2008; and, Richard Leiby, "Tangled U.S. Objectives Bring Down Spy Firm; Private Agents Snared Afghan Drug Kingpin, *Washington Post*, December 27, 2008.

[75] *CBS Evening News*, "Newly Arrived US Army Soldiers Find it Difficult to Adjust...," February 7, 2002; Mark Corcoran, "America's Blind Eye," Australian Broadcasting Corporation, *Foreign Correspondent*, April 10, 2002; and, Steve Inskeep, "Afghanistan's Opium Trade," National Public Radio, April 26, 2002.

[76] U.S. v. Bashir Noorzai, U.S. District Court, Southern District of New York, S1 05 Cr. 19, April 25, 2005.

[77] U.S. v. Baz Mohammed, U.S. District Court, Southern District of New York, S14 03 Cr. 486, October 25, 2005.

[78] U.S. v. Haji Juma Khan, U.S. District Court, Southern District of New York, S1 08 Cr. 621, October 24, 2008.

Opium Profits and Afghanistan's Economic Recovery

Reports continue to indicate that profits from Afghanistan's opium trade may be undermining efforts to reestablish a functioning, licit economy. According to the UNODC/MCN 2008 opium survey, the export value of the 2007-2008 opium harvest, an estimated $3.4 billion, was equal in value to 33% of the country's licit GDP. The World Bank reports that the opium economy has produced significant increases in rural wages and income and remains a significant source of credit for low income rural households. Opium profits fuel consumption of domestic products and support imports of high value goods such as automobiles and appliances from abroad. Funds from the drug trade are also a major source of investment for infrastructure development projects, including major projects in "building construction, trade, and transport."[79] In February 2005, the IMF warned that short term counternarcotics efforts, if successful, had the potential to "adversely affect GDP growth, the balance of payments, and government revenue" by lowering drug income and weakening its support for domestic consumption and taxed imports.[80] In February 2008, the IMF reported that the narcotics trade "continues to be a major obstacle for Afghanistan to regain its comparative advantage in traditional exports."[81]

Trafficking and Consumption Markets

Afghan opium presents significant public health and internal security challenges to downstream markets where refined heroin and other opiates are consumed, including the United States. Russia and Europe have been the main consumption markets for Afghan opiates since the early 1990s, and estimates place Afghan opium as the source of over 90% of the heroin that enters the United Kingdom and Western Europe annually. Russian and European leaders have expressed concern over the growth of Afghanistan's opium trade as both a national security threat as well as a threat to public health and safety.

Trafficking to the United States

Heroin originating in southwest Asia (Afghanistan, Pakistan, Iran, and Turkey) "was the predominant form of heroin available in the United States" from 1980 to 1987.[82] However, the DEA's analysis of data from its Heroin Signature Program and Heroin Domestic Monitor Program indicate that "despite significant increased opium production in Afghanistan, the availability of Southwest Asian heroin in the United States will remain at stable, low levels in the near term."[83] Since the 1980s, several figures involved in the Afghan drug trade have been

---

[79] World Bank, State Building..., p. 87.

[80] International Monetary Fund, IMF Country Report No. 05/33 - Islamic State of Afghanistan: 2004 Article IV Consultation and Second Review, February 2005.

[81] International Monetary Fund, IMF Country Report No. 08/76 - Islamic State of Afghanistan: 2007 Article IV Consultation and Third Review – Staff Report, February 2008, p. 7.

[82] Drug Enforcement Agency (DEA), "The Availability of Southwest Asian Heroin in the United States," May 1996.

[83] DEA, "The Availability of Southwest Asian Heroin in the United States: A Market Analysis," March 7, 2007

convicted of trafficking illegal drugs, including heroin, into the United States.[84] Afghan and Pakistani nationals have been indicted and convicted on heroin trafficking and money laundering charges in U.S. courts in recent years. Since 2001, DEA and FBI investigators have prosecuted several Afghan and Pakistani nationals in connection with heroin trafficking and money laundering charges, including members of Pakistan's Afridi clan.[85] Officials have indicated that some of the individuals involved in these recent cases may have relationships with Taliban insurgents and members of Al Qaeda.[86] Al Qaeda operatives and sympathizers have been captured trafficking large quantities of heroin and hashish and allegedly attempting to trade drugs for Stinger missiles.[87]

Russia

Afghan opiates have been a concern for Russian leaders since the 1980s, when Afghan drug dealers targeted Soviet troops and many Russian soldiers returned from service in Afghanistan addicted to heroin.[88] More recently, the Russian government has expressed deep concern about "narco-terrorist" linkages that are alleged to exist between Chechen rebel groups, their Islamist extremist allies, and Caucasian criminal groups that traffic and distribute heroin in Russia. Since 1993, HIV infection and heroin addiction rates have skyrocketed in Russia, and these trends have been linked to the influx and growing use of Afghan opiates. These concerns make the Afghan narcotics trade an issue of priority interest to Russian decision makers, and motivate attention and initiative on the part of Russian security services in the region. Russia's Federal Drug Control Service (FSKN) serves as its lead agency for counternarcotics and participates in multilateral initiatives to stem the flow of Afghan opiates and counteract shipments of precursor chemicals to Afghanistan and neighboring countries. FSKN forces frequently intercept multi-hundred kilogram shipments of Afghan opiates, and participate in a bi-annual regional seizure operation known as Operation Canal along with counterparts from Armenia, Belarus, Kazakhstan, Kyrgyzstan, Uzbekistan, and Tajikistan.

Western Europe

In Europe, press outlets and public officials in several countries have devoted significant attention to Afghanistan's opium trade since the 1990s. In the United Kingdom, where British officials estimate that 90-95% of the heroin that enters the country annually is derived from Afghan opium, the public places a high priority on combating the Afghan opiate trade. In October 2001, British Prime Minister Tony Blair cited the Taliban regime's tolerance for opium cultivation and

---

[84] In 1985, the DEA developed evidence against a wealthy Afghan national alleged to have been "involved in supplying Afghan rebels with weapons in exchange for heroin and hashish, portions of which were eventually distributed in Western Europe and the United States." See Select Committee on Narcotics Abuse and Control - Annual Report 1985, December 19, 1986, p. 58; See U.S. v. Roeffen, et al. [U.S. District Court of New Jersey (Trenton), 86-00013-01] and U.S. v. Wali [860 F.2d 588 (3d Cir.1988)].

[85] U.S. v. Afridi, et. al., [U.S. District Court of Maryland, (Baltimore), AW-03-0211].

[86] Testimony of DEA Administrator Karen Tandy before the House International Relations Committee, February 12, 2004.

[87] James W. Crawley, "U.S. Warships Pinching Persian Gulf Drug Trade," *San Diego Union-Tribune*, February 9, 2004, and Tony Perry, "2 Convicted of Seeking Missiles for Al Qaeda Ally," *Los Angeles Times*, March 4, 2004.

[88] Defense Department officials report that steps are taken to educate U.S. troops serving in Afghanistan about the dangers of narcotics use and to monitor and prevent drug use. Testimony of Lt. Gen. Walter L. Sharp, Director of Strategic Plans (J-5), Before the House International Relations Committee, September 23, 2004.

---

heroin production as one justification for the United Kingdom's involvement in the U.S.-led military campaign in Afghanistan. Some British citizens and officials have criticized UK counternarcotics efforts in Afghanistan and argued that more should be done to stem the flow of Afghan opiates in the future.[89] The United Kingdom served as the lead nation for international counternarcotics efforts in Afghanistan under the Bonn Accord arrangements, and British government officials assist Afghan counternarcotics authorities in intelligence gathering and targeting operations for interdiction and eradication. British defense officials have deployed 8,900 British troops to participate in the NATO-led International Security Assistance Force (ISAF), many of whom are serving in the key southern opium-producing province of Helmand, where their mission includes efforts to support counternarcotics operations.

Regional Security Implications

Afghanistan's opiate trade presents a range of policy challenges for Afghanistan's neighbors, particularly for the Central Asian republics of the former Soviet Union. As a security issue, regional governments face the challenge of securing their borders and populations against the inflow of Afghan narcotics and infiltration by armed trafficking and terrorist groups. Regional terrorist organizations and international criminal syndicates that move Afghan opiates throughout the region have been linked to insecurity, corruption, and violence in several countries.[90] As a public health issue, Afghan narcotics have contributed to a dramatic upsurge in opiate use and addiction rates in countries neighboring Afghanistan, a factor that also has been linked to dramatic increases in HIV infection rates in many of Afghanistan's neighbors. According to the UNODC, by 2001, "Afghan opiates represented: almost 100% of the illicit opiates consumed in … Iran, Pakistan, Turkey, Kazakhstan, Turkmenistan, Kyrgyzstan, Tajikistan, Uzbekistan, Azerbaijan, and the Russian Federation."[91] With the exception of Turkey, intravenous use of Afghan opiates is a dominant driver of HIV infection rates in each of these countries.[92] These destabilizing factors could provide a powerful pretext for increased attention to and possible intervention in Afghan affairs on the part of regional powers such as Russia, Iran, and Pakistan.

Central and South Asia[93]

The emergence of the so-called "Northern Route" of opiate trafficking through Central Asia and the Caucasus in the mid-1990s transformed the region's previously small and relatively self-contained opiate market into the center of global opium and heroin trafficking. Ineffective border control, civil war, and corruption facilitated this trend, and opiate trafficking and use in

---

[89] House of Commons (UK) - Foreign Affairs Committee, Seventh Report, July 21, 2004.

[90] See Tamara Makarenko, "Crime, Terror and the Central Asian Drug Trade," *Harvard Asia Quarterly*, vol. 6, no. 3 (Summer 2002); and, Integrated Regional Information Networks (IRIN) Report, "Central Asia: Regional Impact of the Afghan Heroin Trade," *U.N. Office for the Coordination of Humanitarian Affairs* (OCHA), August 2004.

[91] UNODC, "The Opium Economy in Afghanistan," p. 33, 35.

[92] For more information, see the World Health Organization's Epidemiological Fact Sheets on HIV/AIDS at http://www.who.int/GlobalAtlas/PDFFactory/HIV/index.asp, and Julie Stachowiak and Chris Beyrer, "HIV Follows Heroin Trafficking Routes," *Open Society Institute - Central Eurasia Project*.

[93] For more on Central Asian security and public health, including information on narcotics trafficking, organized crime, and terrorism see CRS Report RL30294, *Central Asia's Security: Issues and Implications for U.S. Interests*, by Jim Nichol and CRS Report RL30970, *Health in Russia and Other Soviet Successor States: Context and Issues for Congress*, by Jim Nichol.

Kazakhstan, Uzbekistan, Turkmenistan, and Kyrgyzstan now pose significant security and public health threats to those countries. In the past, U.S. officials have implicated the Islamic Movement of Uzbekistan in the regional drug trade, as well as well-organized and heavily armed criminal syndicates that threaten U.S. interests. Under an initiative led by the UNODC, security officials from Azerbaijan, Kazakhstan, Kyrgyzstan, Tajikistan, Turkmenistan and Uzbekistan have agreed to establish a Central Asian Regional Information and Coordination Center (CARICC) to serve as a clearing house for operational coordination and intelligence sharing for counternarcotics and other transnational criminal enforcement efforts.[94]

Tajikistan

Tajikistan has emerged as the primary transit point for Afghan opiates entering Central Asia and being trafficked beyond. The 2009 U.S. State Department INCSR reports that a joint Tajik-Chinese government study of narcotics trafficking in Tajikistan in 2007 estimated that "3 percent of narcotics transiting Tajikistan go to the United States." From 1998 to 2003, Tajikistan's Drug Control Agency seized 30 MT of drugs and narcotics, including 16 MT of heroin. U.N. authorities estimate that the European street value of the 5,600 kg of heroin seized by Tajik authorities in 2003 was over $3 billion.[95] The 201st Russian Army Division stationed troops along the Afghan-Tajik border to disrupt the activities of criminals, narcotics traffickers, and terrorist groups from 1993 through late 2004. Tajik and Russian authorities completed efforts to replace these Russian military forces with Tajik border security guards in August 2005. Russian counternarcotics officials have reported increases in narcotics smuggling via the Tajik-Afghan border following the replacement of the Russian border guards. Tajik officials deny the claims and have announced large-scale seizures since the handover.[96] The State Department has expressed concern about narcotics related corruption in Tajikistan as recently as March 2009, when it warned:

> "The Tajik Government is committed to fighting narcotics; however, corruption within the Tajik government continues to limit the effectiveness of counternarcotics efforts. Corrupt officials at all levels thwart law enforcement efforts as officers strive to move drug investigations up the chain of organized criminal groups. So far, no anti-corruption efforts by the Government of Tajikistan have had a significant impact on the corruption problem."

Pakistan

According to the State Department's 2009 INCSR, Pakistan is a transit country "for opiates and hashish moving to markets around the world and precursor chemicals moving into neighboring Afghanistan." Trafficking groups routinely use western areas of Afghanistan and Pakistan as staging areas for the movement of opiates into and through Iran. Efforts to control the narcotics trade in Pakistan have historically been complicated by the government's limited ability to assert authority over autonomous tribal zones, although recent cooperative border security efforts with the United States have increased the presence of government authorities in these regions and improved opiate seizures. According to INCSR reports, the Pakistani government's efforts to reduce opium poppy cultivation and heroin production since 2001 have been moderately

---

[94] For more information, see the CARICC home page at: http://www.caricc.org/index.php?lang=english.

[95] IRIN Report, "Tajikistan: Stemming the Heroin Tide," OCHA, September 13, 2004. Available at http://www.irinnews.org/webspecials/opium/regTaj.asp.

[96] U.S. Department of State, International Narcotics Control Strategy Report 2006, "Russia," March 2006.

successful. However, the State Department considers Pakistan "a major narcotics producing country with cultivation of poppy still over 1000 hectares."

In March 2003, former U.S. Ambassador to Pakistan Wendy Chamberlain told a House International Relations Committee panel that the role of Pakistan's Inter-Services Intelligence (ISI) agency in the heroin trade from 1997-2003 had been "substantial."[97] The 2009 INCSR stated that the U.S. government "has no evidence that the [government of Pakistan] or any of its senior officials encourage or facilitate" narcotics trafficking and related money laundering. The report notes that because of low salaries for some officials, the fact that corruption occurs is "not surprising." The 2006 INCSR stated that corruption "is likely to be associated with the movement of large quantities of narcotics and pre-cursor chemicals."

Iran

Narcotics trafficking and use continue to present serious security and public health risks to Iran, which, according to the State Department, serves as the transit route for "perhaps 60 percent" of the opiates smuggled from Afghanistan. According to the UNODC 2008 World Drug Report, 37% of all opiates seized worldwide during 2006 were seized in Iran, including 81% of the world's reported opium seizures and 19% of reported global heroin seizures. Although reported seizure rates may not directly correspond with total trafficking volume, seizure patterns suggest that large shipments of opiates entering Iran from Afghanistan and Pakistan are trafficked onward through Turkey to Eastern Europe, over the Caspian Sea into the Black Sea region, and through the Persian Gulf countries into Africa and beyond. Estimates suggest that up to 67% of HIV infections in Iran are related to intravenous drug use by some of the country's more than 3 million estimated opiate users.

To bolster seizure operations, the State Department reports that Iran sharply increased the number of personnel involved in drug interdiction in 2007, from 30,000 law enforcement officers to 50,000, and improved the technical sophistication of its counter-drug detection equipment to include unmanned surveillance vehicles, real-time commercial satellite imagery, and night vision equipment. Iran's interdiction efforts along its eastern borders with Afghanistan and Pakistan are widely credited with forcing opiate traffickers to establish and maintain the "Northern Route" through Central Asia.

The 2008 U.S. Department of State INCSR cited "overwhelming evidence of Iran's strong commitment" to counternarcotics programs, including interdiction and demand reduction. Iran claims to have invested upward of $1 billion to develop an "elaborate series of earthworks, forts and deep trenches to channel potential drug smugglers to areas where they can be confronted and defeated by Iranian security forces." Iran further claims that over 3,500 Iranian security personnel have been killed in clashes with heavily-armed narcotics trafficking groups over the last twenty years, although the State Department has reported that these figures may include personnel killed in counterinsurgency operations against Baluch separatists or other law enforcement operations

---

[97] Ambassador Wendy Chamberlain, "Transcript: Hearing of the Subcommittee on Asia and the Pacific of the House International Relations Committee," Federal News Service, March 20, 2003. See also, Ahmed Rashid, Taliban, Yale University Press, 2000, pp. 120-2, and Barnett Rubin, The Fragmentation of Afghanistan, Yale University Press, 2002, pp. 197-8. See also Rubin, Testimony Before the House Foreign Affairs Subcommittee on Europe and the Middle East and Asian and Pacific Affairs, March 7, 1990.

against non-drug related organized criminal groups. Iranian press outlets regularly feature stories announcing multiple-ton seizures of opiates and armed clashes with traffickers.

Although the absence of bilateral diplomatic relations prevents the United States from directly supporting counternarcotics initiatives in Iran, the 2009 INSCR indicated that the United States and Iran "have worked together productively" in multilateral settings such as the Paris Pact group[98] and formerly in the "Six Plus Two"[99] group. The report further credits Iran with taking "strong measures against illicit narcotics, particularly interdiction of drugs moving into and through its territory," and recognizes Iran as "one of the biggest victims of the recent increase in opium/heroin production" in Afghanistan. Shared interest in interdiction reportedly has led the United Kingdom, France, and Italy to support the Iranian government's counternarcotics efforts by providing grants for security equipment purchases, including bullet-proof vests, four wheel drive vehicles, and night vision equipment for Iran's border patrol guards.[100] Iran does not participate in the U.S.-led Operation Containment initiative, which seeks to place a "security belt" around Afghanistan to prevent chemicals used in converting opium to heroin from entering the country and opium and heroin from leaving. At a March 2009 summit on Afghanistan, Secretary of State Hillary Clinton reportedly responded favorably to a presentation on counternarcotics made by an Iranian delegate, stating that "the issue of counter-narcotics is a worry that we share. We will look for ways to co-operate with them on that. This is a promising sign that there will be future co-operation."[101]

Afghan and U.S. Counternarcotics Policies

The Bonn Agreement that established the Afghan Interim Authority in 2001 committed Afghanistan's new government to cooperation with the international community "in the fight against terrorism, drugs and organized crime."[102] Since taking office in early 2002 and following his election as president in 2004, President Hamid Karzai and his administration have worked to combat the growth of the Afghan narcotics trade by criminalizing poppy cultivation and drug trafficking, outlining a national counternarcotics strategy, extending limited development assistance, and establishing institutions and forces tasked with eradicating poppy crops, interdicting drug traffic, and prosecuting drug criminals. The Afghan National Drug Control Strategy issued in 2003 and updated in 2006 sets goals and guidelines for Afghanistan's counternarcotics initiatives. Those goals have been incorporated into the Afghan National Development Strategy (ANDS),[103] and the international Joint Coordination Monitoring Board (JCMB) monitors the implementation of counternarcotics programs.

---

[98] The UNODC sponsored Paris Pact Initiative provides a venue for law enforcement coordination for countries affected by trafficking and consumption of Afghan opiates. More information available at: https://www.paris-pact.net/.

[99] The "Six Plus Two" group was an informal group of Afghanistan's neighbors - Iran, Pakistan, Tajikistan, Turkmenistan, China, and Uzbekistan plus Russia and the United States. The group met informally from 1999 through 2001. In September 2000, the group adopted a Regional Action Plan to address the narcotics trade in Afghanistan and the region. Available at: http://www.unodc.org/uzbekistan/en/actionplan.html.

[100] Jason Barnes, "The Desert Village that Feeds UK's Heroin Habit," *The Observer* (UK), December 12, 1999; and, John Daniszewski, "Iran's Own Desert Storm," *Los Angeles Times*, March 21, 2000.

[101] Julian Borger, "Iran's offer of help to rebuild Afghanistan heralds new age of diplomacy with the US," *The Guardian* (UK), April 1, 2009.

[102] The Bonn Agreement, December 5, 2001.

[103] Counternarcotics is highlighted as a so-called "cross-cutting issue" in the ANDS. See Afghanistan National (continued...)

Since 2001, the United States and other international partners have contributed billions of dollars to support funding, equipment, forces, and training for various counternarcotics programs in Afghanistan, including interdiction, poppy eradication, economic development, demand reduction, public information, and judicial reform. To date, limited coordination and inconsistent implementation has hindered the effectiveness of counternarcotics assistance and programs. Over time, symbiotic relationships between insecurity, corruption, and narcotics production have proven particularly difficult to disrupt, and, in some areas, such as Helmand, these relationships have become entrenched and prevented the introduction of comprehensive counternarcotics initiatives. Although the large-scale expansion of poppy cultivation and opiate production is a relatively recent phenomenon, most observers and officials now expect that a long-term, sustained international effort will be necessary to sustainably reduce the threat posed by the Afghan opium economy to the security and stability of Afghanistan and the international community.

Afghan Counternarcotics Policies, Programs, and Forces

Bans, Prohibitions, and Policy Statements

Among the first acts of the newly established Afghan Interim Authority created by the Bonn Agreement was the issuance of a decree that banned the opium poppy cultivation, heroin production, opiate trafficking, and drug use on January 17, 2002. On April 3, 2002, Afghan authorities released a second decree that described the scope and goals of an eradication program designed to destroy a portion of the opium poppy crop that had been planted during late 2001. In order to prevent further cultivation during the autumn 2002 planting season, the government issued a third, more specific decree in September 2002 that spelled out plans for the enforcement of bans on opium cultivation, production, trafficking, and abuse. In 2005, the government issued a new counternarcotics law to clarify administrative authorities for counternarcotics policy and to establish clear procedures for investigating and prosecuting major drug offenses. Religious leaders also have spoken out adamantly against involvement in the drug trade. Islamic leaders from Afghanistan's General Council of Ulema issued a *fatwa* or religious ruling in August 2004 that declared poppy cultivation to be contrary to Islamic *sharia* law.[104]

Afghan authorities developed a National Drug Control Strategy (NDCS) in 2003 in consultation with experts and officials from the United States, the United Kingdom, and the UNODC.[105] The strategy declared the Afghan government's commitment to reducing opium poppy cultivation by 70% by 2008 and to completely eliminating poppy cultivation and drug trafficking by 2013. In 2005, the Afghan government released an implementation plan for the strategy that outlined specific initiatives planned in five policy areas, as well as for regional cooperation, eradication, and public information campaigns.[106]

(...continued)

Development Strategy – Cross Cutting Issues: Counter Narcotics Strategy, March 2008. Available at: http://www.ands.gov.af/ands/final_ands/src/final/sector_strategies/Counter%20Narcotics%20Strategy%20-%20English.pdf.

[104] "Afghan Religious Scholars Urge End To Opium Economy," *Associated Press*, August 3, 2004.

[105] Transitional Islamic State of Afghanistan, National Drug Control Strategy, May 18, 2003.

[106] Islamic Republic of Afghanistan, The 1384 (2005) Counter Narcotics Implementation Plan, February 16, 2005.

In January 2006, the Afghan government released an update of the NDCS to incorporate changes in the structure of the government and lessons learned from previous counternarcotics efforts and interagency and inter-governmental initiatives. [107] Unlike the original NDCS, the latest version refrains from setting firm elimination targets or deadlines and identifies more general, overarching goals. The fundamental objective, as outlined in the updated strategy, is "to secure a sustainable decrease in cultivation, production, trafficking, and consumption of illicit drugs with a view to complete and sustainable elimination." Four priority areas outlined in the report focus on the disruption of the drug trade (including high-level traffickers), the strengthening and diversification of legal rural livelihoods, the reduction of the demand for and consumption of illegal drugs, and the development of central and provincial level counternarcotics institutions. As noted above, those priorities are reflected in the Afghan National Development Strategy.[108]

Institutions and Forces

In October 2002, then-Interim President Hamid Karzai announced that the Afghan National Security Council would take responsibility for counternarcotics policy and would oversee the creation and activities of a new Counternarcotics Directorate (CND). The CND subsequently established functional units to analyze data and coordinate action in five areas: judicial reform, law enforcement, alternative livelihood development, demand reduction, and public awareness. Following its establishment in late 2002, the CND worked with other Afghan ministries, local leaders, and international authorities to develop counternarcotics policies and coordinate the creation of counternarcotics institutions and the training of effective personnel. The CND was transformed into a new Ministry of Counternarcotics (MCN) in December 2004. Habibullah Qaderi resigned as Afghanistan's Minister for Counternarcotics in July 2007. Former deputy minister General Khodaidad served as acting minister and was appointed and confirmed as minister in March 2008.

According to the updated NDCS and ANDS, the MCN is responsible for coordinating the government's counternarcotics policies and for gathering and analyzing data on the production, trafficking, consumption, and targeting of narcotics. However, the MCN does not have implementing authorities or agencies and relies on other ministries, primarily the Ministry of Interior for enforcement support.[109] Other relevant ministries include the Ministries of Agriculture, Rural Rehabilitation and Development, Justice, National Defense, Education, Foreign Affairs, Provincial Administrations, Finance, and Information.

Counternarcotics enforcement activities have been directed from within the Ministry of Interior since 2002. General Mohammed Daud was named Deputy Ministry of Interior for Counternarcotics in December 2004. General Daud and his staff work with U.S. and British officials in implementing the Afghan government's expanded counternarcotics enforcement plan.

---

[107] Islamic Republic of Afghanistan - Ministry of Counternarcotics, National Drug Control Strategy: An Updated Five-Year Strategy for Tackling the Illicit Drug Problem, January 2006.

[108] Counternarcotics is highlighted as a so-called "cross-cutting issue". See Afghanistan National Development Strategy – Cross Cutting Issues: Counter Narcotics Strategy, March 2008. Available at: http://www.ands.gov.af/ands/final_ands/src/final/sector_strategies/Counter%20Narcotics%20Strategy%20-%20English.pdf

[109] According to the State Department, the MCN "has less political influence and fewer resources than other government agencies (especially MOI or MOD), and therefore, depends heavily on their support to execute the policy." INCSR 2009.

In November 2006, the World Bank and UNODC warned that a lack of progress in reforming the Ministry of Interior in relation to other ministries such as the Ministry of Defense left Afghan police and counternarcotics officials more vulnerable to corruption.[110] In October 2008, President Karzai replaced Interior Minister Zarrar Moqbel (a Tajik) with Muhammad Hanif Atmar (a Pashtun) and tasked Minister Atmar with working to combat corruption in the police forces and ministries. The Ministry of Interior and Ministry of Defense supervise the following Afghan counternarcotics law enforcement and military entities:

- **Counternarcotics Police-Afghanistan (CNP-A).** The CNP-A consists of investigative and enforcement divisions whose officers work closely with U.S. and British counternarcotics authorities. CNP-A officers continue to receive U.S. training and equipment to support their ability to plan and execute counternarcotics activities independently. Current plans call for the expansion of the Counternarcotics Police Afghanistan (CNP-A) to 2,900 personnel by 2010.

- **National Interdiction Unit (NIU).** The NIU was established as an elite element of the CNP-A in October 2004 and continues to conduct raids across Afghanistan. Several NIU 50-member teams have received U.S. training and officers now operate in cooperation with DEA Foreign Advisory Support Teams (FAST teams, for more see below). According to the State Department, "during 2008, the NIU was capable of conducting its own operations, including requesting and executing search and arrest warrants."

- **Sensitive Investigations Unit/Technical Intercept Unit (TIU)** The SIU and TIU gather evidence via judicially authorized investigations of prominent narcotics targets using a variety of methods including undercover operations and communications intercepts. The evidence supports prosecutions by the criminal justice task force and the central narcotics tribunal (see "Judicial Reform" below). According to the State Department, in 2008, "the SIU was able to independently initiate and complete investigative and undercover cases."

- **Central Eradication Planning Cell (CPEC).** The CPEC is a U.K.-supported targeting and intelligence center that uses sophisticated technology and surveying to target poppy crops and monitor the success of eradication operations. The CPEC provides target data for the Poppy Eradication Force (PEF).

- **Poppy Eradication Force (PEF).** The PEF conducts ground-based eradication of poppy crops based on targeting data provided by the Central Eradication Planning Cell (CPEC). The force is made up of approximately 800 trained eradicators and is supported by security personnel. Afghan and U.S. officials have prioritized so-called "governor-led" eradication efforts supported by joint U.S.-Afghan advisory teams since 2006, after the PEF failed to meet its targets for 2005. Nevertheless, PEF operations have continued and have met significant armed resistance in some areas resulting in casualties. In 2009, PEF operations are expected to expand with security support from a special Afghan National Army unit working in conjunction with Ministry of Interior officials.

- **Counternarcotics Infantry Kandak (CNIK).** In order to expand centrally planned and executed forced eradication to insecure areas of southern

---

[110] Buddenberg and Byrd (eds.). *Afghanistan's Drug Industry.* World Bank/UNODC, November 2006.

Afghanistan, the U.S. military has supported the development of a counternarcotics infantry *kandak* (CNIK) in the Afghan National Army to provide military perimeter security for AEF and other Afghan counternarcotics force missions. It was scheduled to enter service in early 2009.

- **Afghan Special Narcotics Force (ASNF).** The elite ASNF, or "Force 333," has received special training from the British military and carries out interdiction missions against high value targets and in remote areas. The U.S. military provides some intelligence and airlift support for the ASNF. According to the Ministry of Counternarcotics, the ASNF destroys approximately 150 MT of opium annually and has raided hundreds of drug laboratories.

- **Afghan Border Police (ABP).** According to the U.S. Department of Defense, as of July 2008, the ABP had "received the least attention, funding, and training" among the constituent forces of the Afghan National Police and were "manned at levels below 50 percent in many areas, ...poorly equipped, and under-resourced." The Department of Defense funds a State Department administered Border Management Initiative that supports, equips, and trains the ABP.

U.S. Policy Initiatives: Transition from the "Five-Pillar" Plan to New Administration Priorities

In spite of continued efforts on the part of Afghan, U.S., and international authorities, the land area used for opium poppy cultivation in Afghanistan and Afghanistan's corresponding opiate output increased substantially from late 2001 through 2007. Although public awareness of government opium poppy cultivation bans and laws outlawing participation in the narcotics trade is widespread, until recently, counternarcotics enforcement activities have been hindered by the Afghan government's tactical inability to carry out nationwide, effective eradication and interdiction campaigns as well as a lack of adequate legal infrastructure to support drug-related prosecutions. In areas where governor-led eradication and enforcement activities have proven successful and security has permitted the introduction of public information campaigns and development assistance, poppy cultivation has declined for the time being. International development agencies have made positive, but limited, efforts to address structural economic issues associated with rural livelihoods and poppy cultivation. Development efforts were not centrally coordinated or linked directly to counternarcotics goals and initiatives until late 2004; their viability and potential for success remain highly dependent on regional security conditions and political will.

Substantial growth in opium poppy cultivation and narcotics trafficking from 2001 through 2004 led U.S. officials, in consultation with their Afghan and coalition partners, to develop a comprehensive plan to support the implementation of Afghanistan's National Drug Control Strategy. The plan evolved from early 2005 through 2009 but remained based on five key elements, or pillars, that mirrored core Afghan initiatives and called for increased interagency and international cooperation.[111] Under the Bush Administration, the five pillars of U.S. counternarcotics policy in Afghanistan were (1) public information, (2) judicial reform, (3) alternative livelihood development, (4) interdiction, and (5) eradication. The Obama

---

[111] David Shelby, "United States to Help Afghanistan Attack Narcotics Industry," *Washington File*, U.S. Department of State, November 17, 2004.

Administration has signaled that efforts in many of the five pillar areas will continue, but with new orientation and initiatives.

In August 2007, the Bush Administration issued a revised strategy to improve the results of existing counternarcotics policies in light of increasing poppy cultivation and opiate production.[112] As a result, FY2008 and FY2009 programs offered expanded financial and development rewards to poppy-free provinces and the introduced new development awards for provinces contributing to significant interdiction or prosecutions. More U.S. resources also were devoted to supporting interdiction and eradication activities.

As discussed above, the Administration has signaled that U.S. support for eradication efforts will be "phased out" and that new priority will be placed on the expansion of agricultural development assistance and the intensification of interdiction efforts aimed at high level, insurgency-linked traffickers.[113] In addition, new efforts to track finances associated with narcotics trafficking and corruption are being instituted within the U.S. interagency community.

Public Information

Afghan and U.S. authorities have initiated public information campaigns to reach out to ordinary Afghans and raise public awareness about the threat of narcotics and the danger of participation in the illegal drug trade.[114] Information campaigns seek to influence Afghan views on the illegality and economic risks of poppy cultivation as well as the public health risks associated with opiate abuse. The efforts build on the Afghan government's public awareness strategy, which enlists local community and religious leaders to support the government's counternarcotics policies and encourages them to speak out in their communities against drug use and involvement the opium trade. As noted above, Islamic leaders from Afghanistan's General Council of Ulema have supported this effort by publicly condemning poppy cultivation and involvement in the drug trade.[115]

Since 2006, joint U.S.-Afghan Counternarcotics Advisory Teams (CNAT), have worked as provincial level advisors and have convened hundreds of counternarcotics meetings between tribal and community leaders and central government officials. These efforts are designed to support governor-led efforts to reduce poppy cultivation at the provincial level. According to the State Department, in 2008, over 100 awareness and outreach meetings were convened across 7 provinces, including Farah, Helmand, Uruzgan, and Kandahar.[116]

UNODC/MCN surveys since 2005 have demonstrated that farmers across Afghanistan are well aware of the government's ban on opium poppy cultivation and that in some areas farmers who have declined to cultivate opium poppy have done so because they fear incarceration or

---

[112] For detailed information see, U.S. Counternarcotics Strategy for Afghanistan, August 2007, available at http://www.state.gov/p/inl/rls/rpt/90561.htm; Principle Deputy Assistant Secretary of State for International Narcotics and Law Enforcement Affairs Schweich News Briefing on the Counternarcotics Situation in Afghanistan, August 29, 2007; and Ambassador William Wood's Remarks at the Third Annual National Counter Narcotics Conference, August 29, 2007.

[113] CRS interview with USAID personnel, Washington, DC, February 24, 2009.

[114] Ibid.

[115] "Afghan Religious Scholars Urge End To Opium Economy," *Associated Press*, August 3, 2004.

[116] U.S. Department of State, International Narcotics Control Strategy Report 2009: Afghanistan, February 24, 2009.

---

government eradication of their crops. UNODC/MCN surveys reported that Islamic prohibitions on involvement with narcotics also was influential among Afghans, particularly those that had not yet been involved with cultivation or trafficking.

Judicial Reform

State Department (INL) and Justice Department personnel are undertaking judicial reform efforts to further enable Afghan authorities to enforce counternarcotics laws and prosecute prominent individuals involved in narcotics trafficking. With U.S. and coalition support, the government of Afghanistan drafted and issued a new counternarcotics law in December 2005 that clarifies administrative authorities for counternarcotics policy and establishes clear procedures for investigating and prosecuting major drug offenses. Since 2006, U.S. officials have called on the Afghan authorities "to start prosecuting corrupt officials" and "to start building cases that will stand up in court" under the new law.[117] Then-Counternarcotics Minister Habibullah Qaderi conceded in September 2006 that, at that time Afghan authorities were "not going after the people who matter," although some observers expect that corrupt officials and higher level narcotics traffickers may be prosecuted under the new law as planned anti-corruption initiatives move forward.

To that end, a Criminal Justice Task Force (CJTF) has been developed and granted jurisdiction over significant narcotics cases under presidential decree. The CJTF features integrated teams of prosecutors and investigators that are being specially trained to handle complex, high-profile cases. U.S. Department of Justice personnel participate in CJTF training and mentoring activities in Afghanistan.[118] The CJTF prepares cases for the Central Narcotics Tribunal (CNT) under the jurisdiction of fourteen specially trained judges. The U.S. Defense Department supported the construction of a secure court facility and has contributed to the construction of a maximum-security wing at the Pol-e Charki prison near Kabul to hold offenders prosecuted by the Task Force. As of February 2009, the CJTF and CNT team included 30 Afghan prosecutors, 35 Afghan criminal investigators, 7 primary court and 7 appellate court judges. The chief judge of the CNT Alim Hanif was murdered in Kabul in September 2008.[119] A dedicated secure facility for the CJTF and CNT known as the Counter Narcotics Justice Center is scheduled to open in 2009, and the State Department plans to support its operations and maintenance costs through FY2011.

To date, Afghan and coalition officials have worked together to identify targets for prosecution, although, according to U.S. officials, political concerns and security conditions are considered in the targeting of individuals. To date, the most high profile cases have been handled with direct assistance from or the transfer of suspects to the United States (see "Traffickers and Criminal Syndicates" above). In July 2008, Attorney General Abdul Jabbar Sabit, who according to the State Department is "an anti-corruption activist" and had been "pursuing corruption

---

[117] Thomas A. Schweich, Principal Deputy Assistant Secretary of State for International Narcotics and Law Enforcement Affairs, quoted in Pamela Constable, "A Poor Yield For Afghans' War on Drugs," *Washington Post*, September 19, 2006.

[118] As of January 2009, six senior Assistant U.S. Attorneys were in Kabul serving as Senior Legal Advisors to the CJTF along with three senior criminal investigators. U.S. Department of Defense, Progress toward Security and Stability in Afghanistan, Report to Congress in accordance with the 2008 National Defense Authorization Act (Section 1230, P.L. 110-181), January 2009, pp. 54-55.

[119] Hamid Shalizi, "Slain Afghan judge had received death threats," *Reuters*, September 5, 2008.

investigations against politically sensitive targets."[120] was fired by President Karzai and replaced by Deputy Attorney General Muhammad Ishaq Aloko. Most outside observers associate Sabit's firing with his announcement of his intention to run for president in Afghanistan's pending election. In October 2008, President Karzai named Hanif Atmar as Interior Minister, a move that U.S. officials consider a signal that corruption within Afghanistan's police and counternarcotics enforcement services will no longer be tolerated.

Alternative Livelihood Development

Three current Alternative Development and Livelihoods (AD) programs (known as AD/South, AD/North, and AD/East), are scheduled to be renewed during 2009, with a fourth program (known as AD/Northwest) continuing through March 2010. As noted above (see "Obama Administration Strategic Review and Funding Requests"), new policy guidelines suggest that agricultural development will be a focal point for the Obama Administration's efforts to expand civilian assistance to Afghanistan.

Since February 2005, the regional AD programs have followed two tracks. First, so-called "immediate needs" and "cash-for-work" programs have sponsored labor-intensive work projects to rehabilitate agricultural infrastructure such as canals while providing non-opium incomes to rural laborers. Second, "comprehensive development" programs accelerated existing agricultural development initiatives and initiated new infrastructure development, credit and financial services expansion, agricultural diversification, and private investment support in urban and rural areas.

According to USAID,[121] from 2002 through the end of 2008 alternative livelihood cash-for-work programs had paid $37 million in salaries to close to 300,000 farmers who otherwise may have engaged in or supported opium poppy cultivation. Over 5,700 km of irrigation canals, drainage ditches, and traditional water transportation systems have been repaired and cleaned in a number of provinces, improving irrigation and supporting high value agriculture on an estimated 250,000 hectares of land. More than 414,000 farmers have received seeds or fertilizer (or both) in conjunction with counternarcotics information across Afghanistan since late 2002. Over 30,000 farmers hold licit crop farming contracts with USAID programs.

> **Helmand: Food Zone Program**
>
> Helmand Governor Gulab Mangal, USAID, and the United Kingdom have developed a targeted alternative development effort in Helmand province known as the "Food Zone" program. The initiative is geared toward low income farmers in a series of zones in the fertile poppy producing areas along the Helmand river covering a 27,000 hectare area that stretches from Gareshk in the north through the provincial capital of Lashkar Gah to Garmsir in the south. The program includes the distribution of improved seeds and fertilizer along with technical assistance during planting, tending, and harvest periods. Beneficiary farmers are required to sign pledges to not grow poppy, and strong eradication efforts have been introduced to areas not participating in the program. Governor Mangal is credited with having led an effective administration as the governor of Laghman Province and is viewed by U.S. officials as committed to achieving counternarcotics goals in Afghanistan's main poppy producing province.

Other USAID programs that support broad alternative development goals include the Accelerating Sustainable Agriculture Program (ASAP), which now is in place in 17 northern central and western provinces, and the Agriculture, Rural Investment, and Enterprise

---

[120] INCSR 2008.

[121] USAID, Alternative Development and Agriculture (ADAG) Office Update, end-FY2008; and, author consultation with USAID Afghanistan Desk Office, February 2009.

Strengthening (ARIES) Project, which seeks to improve access to lending in rural areas of all 34 Afghan provinces. In addition, the State Department administered "Good Performer's Initiative" has delivered millions of dollars in targeted economic assistance, including agricultural assistance, to provinces that have met poppy cultivation reduction targets.

USAID and State Department project managers consult with national, provincial, and local authorities, whose planning input varies by program. In some cases, local Community Development Councils select laborers and projects in support of Afghan Provincial Development Plans. Accountability standards have been built into the USAID alternative livelihood programs, including seed and fertilizer distributions and cash-for-work programs. Seed and fertilizer recipients, including government officials, are required to agree in writing not to grow poppy in exchange for program support. Cash-for-work program participants must make similar commitments, and program staff monitor participant activities outside of the program to ensure compliance. According to USAID, all alternative livelihood program assistance is 100% conditional on the reduction of poppy cultivation within one year of the receipt of assistance.[122]

Interdiction

Reflecting on the initial absence of effective counternarcotics institutions and authorities in immediate post-Taliban Afghanistan, international authorities led by the United States Drug Enforcement Administration (DEA) established a series of cooperative interdiction initiatives in countries neighboring Afghanistan beginning in early 2002. The primary U.S.-led effort, known as "Operation Containment," is designed to "implement a joint strategy to deprive drug trafficking organizations of their market access and international terrorist groups of financial support from drugs, precursor chemicals, weapons, ammunition and currency."[123] Operation Containment has continued since early 2002 and currently involves "nineteen countries from Central Asia, the Caucasus, Europe and Russia."[124] A similar multinational DEA-led effort named Operation Topaz has focused on interdicting acetic anhydride—a primary heroin production precursor chemical—to Afghanistan.

The DEA has significantly expanded its presence in Afghanistan since January 2003. DEA Foreign Advisory and Support Teams (FAST) have been deployed to Afghanistan "to provide guidance and conduct bilateral investigations that will identify, target, and disrupt illicit drug trafficking organizations." The FAST teams receive Defense Department transportation and construction support and are currently conducting operations and serving as mentors to officers of the Afghan National Interdiction Unit (NIU). The DEA received new FY2006 funding to expand its operational presence in Afghanistan and Central Asia, including support for FAST teams, Operation Containment activities, and new field officers. Under the Bush Administration, plans were developed to increase the resources devoted to interdiction efforts, including to expand the number of DEA personnel in Afghanistan to over 50 agents and staff. As of March 2009, 13 DEA agents and 3 pilots were present in Afghanistan.[125]

---

[122] Author consultation with USAID Afghanistan Desk Office, January 2006.

[123] DEA Administrator Karen P. Tandy, House Committee on Government Reform Subcommittee on Criminal Justice, Drug Policy and Human Resources, February 26, 2004.

[124] Ibid.

[125] Testimony of Acting DEA Administrator Michelle Leonhart before the House Appropriations Subcommittee On Commerce, Justice, Science, and Related Agencies Hearing on the Drug Enforcement Administration, March 26, 2009.

Defense Department directives once stated that U.S. military forces in Afghanistan did not and would not directly target drug production facilities or pursue drug traffickers as a distinct component of ongoing U.S. counternarcotics initiatives.[126] Rules of engagement allowed U.S. forces to seize and destroy drugs and drug infrastructure discovered during the course of routine military operations carried out in pursuit of conventional counterterrorism and stability missions.[127] Those rules of engagement reportedly have been changed, but the Defense Department is not making public any details on the content of reported changes.[128] Under new NATO/ISAF agreements, some coalition participants, including the United States, have agreed to target narcotics traffickers and infrastructure linked to the Taliban and other insurgent elements.

Defense Department policy guidance issued in December 2008 states that Department personnel "will not directly participate in searches, seizures, arrests, or similar activity unless such personnel are otherwise authorized by law" with the exception of the provision of force protection "up to and including on the objective."[129] According to the guidance, Department personnel may accompany U.S. or host nation law enforcement and security forces on counternarcotics field operations within presidentially declared combat zones. U.S. initiatives that supply Afghan police with tents, boots, communication equipment, mobility support, infrastructure improvements, and training are expected to continue, subject to congressional authorization.

Eradication

The expansion of opium poppy cultivation through 2007 was cited by officials and observers as evidence that centrally planned and executed manual eradication campaigns were failing to serve as a credible deterrent for Afghan farmers. Plans developed by the State Department, in consultation with Afghan authorities, called for early and more robust opium poppy eradication measures for the 2004-2005 growing season to provide a strong deterrent to future cultivation. The Afghan Central Poppy Eradication Force (CPEF) carried out limited operations with support from U.K. intelligence officers, U.S. advisors, and international contractors in early 2005. Field reports indicated that CPEF personnel met violent resistance from farmers in some instances and largely failed to meet their eradication targets for the 2004-2005 season.[130] State Department officials identified the failure of 2004-2005 eradication activities as one factor behind the surge in poppy cultivation that occurred during the 2005-2006 season, and made similar judgments with regard to the 2006-2007 crop.

From 2006 to 2008, the United States shifted its efforts toward advising and rewarding governor-led eradication programs, while seeking to improve the performance and security of national eradication teams. At the provincial level, Afghan and coalition advisors helped direct and monitor locally led and administered eradication efforts and assisted in organizing supporting activities such as public information campaigns and public consultation sessions. At the national level, policy efforts have focused on creating enhanced security capabilities for eradication

---

[126] Defense Department response to CRS inquiry, November 12, 2004.

[127] Testimony of Thomas W. O'Connell, Assistant Secretary of Defense for Special Operations and Low-intensity Conflict Before House International Relations Committee, February 12, 2004; and Defense Department response to CRS inquiry, November 12, 2004.

[128] Author consultation with Department of Defense officials, February 2009.

[129] U.S. Department of Defense, Memorandum: Department of Defense International Counternarcotics Policy, December 24, 2008.

[130] Author conversation with DEA official, Washington, DC, May 2005.

forces, culminating in the introduction of the Counternarcotics Infantry Kandak in early 2009 to protect eradication teams inserted into hostile areas. According to UNODC, "eradication activities in 2008 were severely affected by resistance from insurgents," and "since most of the poppy cultivation remains confined to the south and south-west region dominated by strong insurgency, eradication operations may in the future become even more challenging."[131]

Table 5. UNODC Poppy Eradication Estimates for Afghanistan, 2005-2008

Area in Hectares

Year	Hectarage Eradicated		Annual Total	Annual % Change	Annual Nationwide Cultivation
	National Forces	Governor Led			
2005	1,105	4,007	5,112	a	104,000
2006	2,250	13,050	15,300	199.0%	165,000
2007	3,149	15,898	19,047	24.5%	193,000
2008	1,174	4,306	5,480	-71.2%	157,000

Source: UNODC/MCN, Afghanistan Opium Surveys, 2005-2008.

Notes: Aggregate eradication estimates provide a general measure of the activity of provincial and national eradication forces. Concentration of eradication in various provinces is not reflected in aggregate data, but is reported by UNODC. Not all reported eradication totals were verified by UNODC and as such some reported area totals are less than annual sum totals reported by governors. Experts consider the location, targeting, and timing of eradication, along with the provision of follow-on assistance or enforcement measures as important indicators of the impact of eradication and its long term effects.

a.   The UNODC did not monitor or report on the limited eradication efforts in the 2004 growing season. In its 2004 report, the UNODC identified the introduction of "a centrally-conducted eradication *cum* persuasion campaign" as a "measurable goal" for the then-new Afghan government.

Bush Administration officials stressed the importance of early season, locally executed eradication in order to minimize violent farmer resistance and give Afghan farmers time to plant licit replacement cash crops. At the same time, the State Department pressed for effective centrally directed and non-negotiable eradication targeted at large scale cultivators. Some field researchers report that in some areas, locally administered eradication results in the targeting of the fields of non-influential and smaller scale landowners and farmers unwilling or unable to secure political protection. New methods and technologies for future eradication activities also have been considered, including the introduction of manual herbicide spraying to improve eradication teams' efficiency. In January 2007, President Karzai announced that any herbicide-based eradication efforts would be delayed (see "Manual or Aerial Herbicide-based Eradication" above). According to Obama Administration officials, U.S. support for eradication efforts in Afghanistan will be "phased out." The effects this will have on the viability and success of any continuing Afghan eradication efforts are uncertain.

---

[131] UNODC/MCN, Afghanistan Opium Survey 2008: Executive Summary, August 2008.

Cited Field Surveys and Research Studies

Doris Buddenberg and William A. Byrd (eds.), *Afghanistan's Drug Industry: Structure, Functioning, Dynamics, and Implications for Counter-Narcotics Policy*, World Bank/UNODC, November 2006.

Jonathan Goodhand, "From Holy War to Opium War: A Case Study of the Opium Economy in North Eastern Afghanistan," Peacebuilding and Complex Emergencies Working Paper Series, No. 5, University of Manchester, 1999.

Frank Kenefick, and Larry Morgan, "Opium in Afghanistan: People and Poppies—The Good Evil," Chemonics International Inc. for USAID, February 5, 2004.

David Mansfield, "Coping Strategies, Accumulated Wealth and Shifting Markets: The Story of Opium Poppy Cultivation in Badakhshan 2000-2003," Agha Khan Development Network, January 2004.

———, "Alternative Development in Afghanistan: The Failure of Quid Pro Quo," International Conference on the Role of Alternative Development in Drug Control and Development Cooperation, January 2002.

———, "Exploring the 'Shades of Grey': An Assessment of the Factors. Influencing Decisions to Cultivate Opium Poppy in 2005/06," Report for the Afghan Drugs Inter-Departmental Unit of the Government of the United Kingdom, December 2005.

———, "Responding to Risk and Uncertainty: Understanding the Nature of Change in the Rural Livelihoods of Opium Poppy Growing Households in the 2007/08 Growing Season," Report for the Afghan Drugs Inter-Departmental Unit of the Government of the United Kingdom, July 2008

David Mansfield and Adam Pain, "Counter-Narcotics in Afghanistan: The Failure of Success?" Afghan Research and Evaluation Unit, December 2008.

———, "Opium Poppy Eradication: How to Raise Risk When There is Nothing to Lose?" Afghan Research and Evaluation Unit, August 2006.

Adam Pain, "'Let Them Eat Promises': Closing the Opium Poppy Fields in Balkh and its Consequences," Afghanistan Research and Evaluation Unit Case Study Series, December 2008.

———, "The Impact of the Opium Poppy Economy on Household Livelihoods: Evidence from the Wakhan Corridor and Khustak Valley in Badakhshan," Aga Kahn Development Network, Badakhshan Programme, January 2004.

UNODC, Strategic Study Series #1-6, June 1998-June 2000.

Christopher Ward, David Mansfield, Peter Oldham and William Byrd, "Afghanistan: Economic Incentives and Development Initiatives to Reduce Opium Production," World Bank and UK Department For International Development, February 5, 2008.

Author Contact Information

Christopher M. Blanchard
Analyst in Middle Eastern Affairs
cblanchard@crs.loc.gov, 7-0428